THE
ALMANAC

THE
ALMANAC
A SEASONAL GUIDE TO
2019

LIA LEENDERTZ

With illustrations by Celia Hart

MITCHELL BEAZLEY

An Hachette UK Company
www.hachette.co.uk

First published in Great Britain in 2018 by Mitchell Beazley,
an imprint of Octopus Publishing Group Ltd
Carmelite House
50 Victoria Embankment
London EC4Y 0DZ
www.octopusbooks.co.uk

ISBN 978-1-78472-515-0

A CIP catalogue record for this book is available from the British Library.

Printed and bound in the United Kingdom

10 9 8 7 6 5 4

Publishing Director: Stephanie Jackson
Creative Director: Jonathan Christie
Designer: Matt Cox at Newman+Eastwood
Junior Editor: Ella Parsons
Copy Editor: Alison Wormleighton
Senior Production Manager: Peter Hunt

Ovens should be preheated to the specific temperature – if using a fan-assisted
oven, follow your oven manufacturer's instructions for adjusting the time
and the temperature. Pepper should be freshly ground black pepper unless
otherwise stated.

CONTENTS

INTRODUCTION

Welcome to *The Almanac: A Seasonal Guide to 2019*. For those who enjoyed last year's edition, this book includes new features to celebrate seasonal songs and folklore, cheeses of the month, meteor showers and beehive behaviour. For newcomers, this book is intended as a toolkit for connecting with the world around you, and the year ahead as it unfolds. It is about the things that will make each month of the coming year feel special – the festivities, gardening, natural phenomena and seasonal foods that mark out that month, as well as the tides, moon phases and sunrise and sunset times that are particular to 2019.

The Almanac offers ways of appreciating the natural rhythms of the year no matter what your energy level or inclination. If you want to get out for a country walk at bluebell time or watch the sunrise at dawn on midsummer's day, then yes, this is the book for you. But if it suits you better to sit at your window and spot Mars alongside the crescent moon (January), or eat strawberries when they are at their peak (June), or learn a harvest song that has been sung for centuries (August), then you will also do well to have this almanac at your side. Maybe you just want to stand on London Bridge at rush hour and know that the tide is at its height. *The Almanac* is as happy on an easy chair's armrest as it is in the kitchen, in the handbag or in the backpack. While I realise it has the potential to spark outings and gatherings, I hope above all that it will prompt a lot of gazing and thinking, because that is what it does for me.

However you use it, I wish you a year of feeling a part of things: of the turning of the earth and the seasons below your feet, the buzzing of the bees and the blooming of the flowers they land on, the arrival of crops, the coming and going of tides, and the moon, sun and planets performing their cosmic dance, just outside the window there.

Have a wonderful 2019.

Lia Leendertz

NOTES ON USING *THE ALMANAC*

Scope

The geographical scope of this almanac is the archipelagos of the British Isles and the Channel Islands or, to put it another way around, Great Britain and Northern Ireland, plus the Isle of Man, the Channel Islands and the Republic of Ireland. 'The British Isles' is used as shorthand, with apologies to the Channel Islands. The cultural scope of this almanac is the stories, songs, food and festivities of all the people who live in the British Isles.

The sky at night

The events within the sky at night sections generally fall into three categories: eclipses; meteor showers; and close approaches of the moon to a naked-eye planet, or of two naked-eye planets to each other. While the first two categories are self-explanatory, the third will benefit from a little clarification. The naked-eye planets are those planets that can be easily seen with the naked eye. They are generally very bright, as bright as the brightest stars, and this makes them relatively easy to spot, even in cities where sky-spotting conditions are not ideal. From brightest to dimmest they are Venus, Jupiter, Mars and Saturn. Those not included in this almanac are Mercury, Neptune and Uranus. Mercury is very hard to spot because it is close to the sun and therefore is usually lost in its glare. Neptune and Uranus can only be spotted with strong telescopes.

A 'close approach' means that two of them, or one of them plus the moon, are in the same part of the sky. They are, of course, nowhere near each other in reality, but to us, looking up, they appear as if they are. This can make them easier to spot than they would be when they are lone-ranging across the sky. To identify the part of the sky where they will most easily be seen, I have given the best time to spot them, plus a compass point and the altitude. The time is important, because the sky wheels around us as the night wears on. The altitude is given in degrees: the horizon is 0 degrees and straight up is 90 degrees, so find your point somewhere in between.

Tides

A full tide timetable is given each month for Dover. For approximate high water time differences for various spots around the coast, refer to the table below. Note that these approximations provide a fairly rough idea of tide times, though generally will be correct within ten minutes or so.

Approximate high water time differences on Dover

Add or subtract these amounts of time from the Dover timetable to find the tide times for the following locations. For instance, if it is high tide at Dover at midday, it will be high tide at Bristol (−4h 10m) at 07.50 and at Aberdeen (+2h 31m) at 14.31.

Aberdeen:	+2h 31m	Cork:	−5h 23m
Firth of Forth:	+3h 50m	Swansea:	−4h 50m
Port Glasgow:	+1h 32m	Bristol:	−4h 10m
Newcastle-upon-Tyne:	+4h 33m	London Bridge:	+2h 52m
Belfast Lough:	+0h 7m	Lyme Regis:	−4h 55m
Hull:	−4h 52m	Newquay:	−6h 4m
Liverpool:	+0h 14m	St Helier, Jersey:	−4h 55m

Do not use these tables where accuracy is critical – you will need to buy a local tide timetable, or subscribe to Easy Tide, www.ukho.gov.uk/easytide. Also note that no timetable will take into account the effects of wind and barometric pressure.

The approximate high water time differences may look quite random. This is because tides do not cause a general raising and lowering of the water all around the British Isles. They work more like a series of huge waves travelling around the coast, the crest of the wave being high tide and the trough of the wave being low tide. One set of waves travels up the west coast of Wales and the east coast of Ireland where they join up with another set coming up Ireland's west coast. They then travel up and over the top of Scotland and part way down the east coast of England. Another set heads off in the opposite direction from Land's End along the south coast of England and up the east coast, where they meet the first set of waves. So there will be tidal peaks and troughs all around the coast at different times: when it is high tide at Land's End it will also be high tide on the west coast of Scotland and in Yorkshire. At the same time it will be low tide in north Wales, the northeast coast of Scotland and the Thames Estuary. Once high tide has passed, low tide will be along in around 6 hours 12 and a half minutes. Using this and the above, you may be able to work out the tide times for where you are.

Spring and neap tide dates are also included. Spring tides are the most extreme of the month – the highest and lowest tides – and neap tides are the least extreme. Spring tides occur as a result of the pull that happens when the sun, moon and earth are aligned. Alignment occurs at new moon and full moon, but the surge – the spring tide – is slightly delayed because of the mass of water to be moved. It usually follows one to three days after. Knowledge of spring tides is useful if you are a keen rock-pooler or mudlarker. You want a low spring tide for best revelations.

Gardening by the moon

Just as the moon moves the earth's water to create tides, some believe that it has other, hidden but equally consequential, effects on the natural world. If it can move the oceans perhaps it can move ground water, too, and even the small amounts trapped in each plant. Planting by the moon is a method of gardening that taps into and utilises the rise and fall of water with the moon's phases. A new moon is considered a good time to sow root and slower-germinating crops, because soil moisture is increasing. Faster-germinating plants that crop above ground should be sown in the run-up to full moon, when the pull is at its strongest and so ground water will be at its highest. The full moon is also the best time to harvest crops for immediate use, as they will be at their juiciest. After that, the moon's pull starts to wane and ground water drops – these are good times for pruning (to minimise sap loss) and harvesting for storage (skins are drier and tougher). This almanac makes no claims on the efficacy of planting by the moon, but if you would like to give it a try you will find relevant dates and jobs in each month.

January

The naming of January

> Faoilleach (Scots Gaelic)
> Januar (Scots/Ulster Scots)
> Eanáir (Irish Gaelic)
> Jerry-gueree (Manx)
> Ionawr (Welsh)
> Genver (Cornish)
> Janvyi (Jèrriais)

The word Faoilleach in Scots Gaelic originally referred to a period of winter, but has come to mean specifically January in modern Scots Gaelic. It comes from *faol-chu* which means 'wolf', and this gives a glimpse into Scotland's wilder past Januarys, as there have been no wolves in Scotland for hundreds of years (the last wolf having been slain by legendary deerstalker MacQueen of Findhorn in 1743). Wolves' howling reaches its height in January in mating season as the males compete for mates, before falling quiet during the denning season. All of the other words for January from the various languages of the British Isles appear to be variants on the Latin *Januarius*. This may have arisen from either the Latin for 'door', *ianua* (the door onto the year), or the Roman god Janus, the god of transitions and beginnings, traditionally depicted as having two faces, one looking back into the past and one looking ahead to the future.

A RASTAFARI STORY FOR JANUARY

Epiphany, Lidat and the Three Kings

Balthazar was the King of Ethiopia. A new and bright star appeared in the sky, as had been foretold in the Star Prophecy: a prediction of the coming of a new Messiah. And so Balthazar gathered myrrh, the precious resin of the small thorny tree *Commiphora myrrha*, which grows in eastern and northern Ethiopia, and set off for Bethlehem with two other great kings – Caspar and Melchior – to pay their respects.

Rastafarians celebrate the birth of Christ, who they believe was black, on 7th January, and call it Lidat, which means 'birthday' in Amharic, the main language of Ethiopia. Rastafari is intricately connected to Christianity but based upon a particular reading of the Bible that centres on its many mentions of Ethiopia, including its role as the 'promised land'. The Ethiopian Orthodox Church is after all one of the oldest churches in the world: Christianity has existed in Ethiopia since AD 330. Rastafari itself is a young religion, originating among impoverished African–Jamaican communities in the 1930s, its Africa-centric vision emerging partly as a reaction to British colonialism and as a way of reclaiming an African identity lost through slavery. Rastas believe that the Bible was originally written in Amharic and is an authentic account of early black history and black Africans' place as God's favoured people, the Israelites, but that this original meaning has been warped by mistranslation to deny black Africans their true history.

This date of 7th January is in tune with the Julian calendar followed by the older Orthodox churches, but Rastas do not insist that this was the actual date of Jesus' birth (merely rejecting the date of the 25th December, which they consider a later construct to convert midwinter-worshipping pagans to Christianity). They do, however, consider this as the date upon which the Magi visited Jesus. A feast is prepared, children are given simple presents and they play games. The main decoration is that of the manger with the three Magi, including the Ethiopian king paying homage to the young black Messiah.

WEATHER

Types of snow
Stellar dentrites: The classic snowflake, with a star-like (stellar) shape, but branched (dentrite). Big, easy to spot and common. The most spectacular form at around −15°C but they will also form when it is warmer.
Graupel: Sometimes called soft hail, sometimes snow pellets, these occur when water droplets collide with snow crystals inside the cloud and freeze onto them.
Needle crystals: Long, columnar crystals that are common but hard to spot as they are so fine. They are formed at around −6°C.
Diamond dust crystals: The smallest of all snow crystals, and most often spotted during bitterly cold weather. They glisten like diamond dust in sunlight.

Average temperatures (°C):	Inverness 4, Padstow 6
Average sunshine hours per day:	Inverness 2, Padstow 2
Average days of rainfall:	Inverness 20, Padstow 25
Average rainfall total (mm):	Inverness 50, Padstow 98

Day length
During the course of January, day length increases by:

1 hour 35 minutes (to 8 hours 19 minutes) – Inverness

1 hour 8 minutes (to 9 hours 13 minutes) – Padstow

Perihelion is on 3rd January at 05.19. This is the moment in the year when the earth is closest to the sun.

Sunrise and set

| | *Inverness* | | *Padstow* | |
	Rise	Set	Rise	Set
1st	08.58	15.42	08.20	16.25
2nd	08.58	15.43	08.20	16.26
3rd	08.57	15.45	08.20	16.27
4th	08.57	15.46	08.20	16.29
5th	08.56	15.48	08.20	16.30
6th	08.55	15.49	08.19	16.31
7th	08.55	15.51	08.19	16.32
8th	08.54	15.52	08.19	16.33
9th	08.53	15.54	08.18	16.35
10th	08.52	15.56	08.18	16.36
11th	08.51	15.58	08.17	16.37
12th	08.50	15.59	08.16	16.39
13th	08.49	16.01	08.16	16.40
14th	08.48	16.03	08.15	16.42
15th	08.47	16.05	08.14	16.43
16th	08.46	16.07	08.14	16.45
17th	08.44	16.09	08.13	16.46
18th	08.43	16.11	08.12	16.48
19th	08.41	16.13	08.11	16.49
20th	08.40	16.15	08.10	16.51
21st	08.38	16.18	08.09	16.53
22nd	08.37	16.20	08.08	16.54
23rd	08.35	16.22	08.07	16.56
24th	08.33	16.24	08.05	16.58
25th	08.32	16.26	08.04	16.59
26th	08.30	16.29	08.03	17.01
27th	08.28	16.31	08.02	17.03
28th	08.26	16.33	08.00	17.04
29th	08.24	16.35	07.59	17.06
30th	08.22	16.38	07.58	17.08
31st	08.20	16.40	07.56	17.10

THE SEA

Average sea temperature

Isle of Lewis:	8.5°C
Whitby:	7.3°C
Belfast:	8.8°C
Cork:	9.8°C
Swansea:	8.8°C
Brighton:	9.2°C
Falmouth:	10.4°C

Spring and neap tides

The spring tides are the most extreme tides of the month, with the highest rises and falls, and the neap tides are the least extreme, with the smallest. Exact timings vary around the coast, but expect them around the following dates:

Spring tides: 8th–9th and 23rd–24th

Neap tides: 15th–16th and 29th–30th

In the tide timetable opposite, spring tides are shown with an asterisk.

January tide timetable for Dover

For your local high tide differences on Dover, see page 8.

	High water		Low water	
	Morning	Afternoon	Morning	Afternoon
1st	07.10	19.55	01.42	14.19
2nd	08.15	20.52	02.51	15.26
3rd	09.12	21.40	03.57	16.29
4th	10.00	22.23	04.54	17.19
5th	10.42	23.01	05.40	18.00
6th	11.20	23.38	06.19	18.35
7th	11.56	–	06.54	19.06
8th	00.14	12.30	07.25	19.34 *
9th	00.48	13.02	07.54	20.04 *
10th	01.18	13.31	08.26	20.36
11th	01.44	13.58	08.59	21.11
12th	02.13	14.30	09.36	21.48
13th	02.50	15.12	10.16	22.30
14th	03.37	16.07	11.03	23.21
15th	04.39	17.28	–	12.04
16th	05.58	18.51	00.32	13.22
17th	07.12	19.54	01.54	14.33
18th	08.13	20.48	03.04	15.37
19th	09.08	21.39	04.05	16.36
20th	09.59	22.28	05.02	17.34
21st	10.49	23.16	05.58	18.30
22nd	11.37	–	06.54	19.24
23rd	00.02	12.24	07.46	20.12 *
24th	00.49	13.12	08.35	20.56 *
25th	01.36	14.00	09.20	21.37
26th	02.25	14.51	10.03	22.18
27th	03.15	15.45	10.47	23.02
28th	04.09	16.44	11.35	23.55
29th	05.10	17.54	–	12.32
30th	06.22	19.11	00.57	13.36
31st	07.43	20.23	02.08	14.44

THE SKY AT NIGHT

Moon phases

New moon – 6th January

1st quarter – 14th January

Full moon – 21st January

3rd quarter – 27th January

Meteor shower of the month – the Quadrantids

The night and pre-dawn hours of 3–4 January bring the peak of the Quadrantids, one of the more generous meteor showers of the year, with up to 40 meteors an hour at its peak (and even the occasional fireball with glowing tail). It is often missed, as the trails are faint and the peak is quick, lasting no more than two hours. However, this year's peak coincides with an almost new moon and a dark sky: perfect spotting conditions. Meteors are pieces of debris entering our planet's atmosphere, vaporising and causing streaks of light, and the Quadrantids occur when the earth annually passes through the dust left behind by the extinct comet (and so now asteroid) 2003 EH1, which passed us five hundred years ago. Meteors will radiate from the constellation Boötes but can appear anywhere in the sky. The best time for viewing will be around 04.00 on the 4th when the radiant will be at an altitude of 50 degrees in the northeast sky.

Moon rise and set

	Inverness		Padstow		
	Rise	Set	Rise	Set	
1st	03.42	13.21	03.27	13.44	
2nd	04.59	13.43	04.37	14.13	
3rd	06.13	14.10	05.44	14.46	
4th	07.21	14.44	06.47	15.25	
5th	08.20	15.27	07.43	16.10	
6th	09.09	16.21	08.33	17.03	new moon
7th	09.47	17.22	09.14	18.00	
8th	10.17	18.29	09.49	19.01	
9th	10.40	19.38	10.18	20.04	
10th	10.58	20.49	10.43	21.08	
11th	11.14	22.00	11.05	22.13	
12th	11.28	23.13	11.25	23.18	
13th	11.41	–	11.45	–	
14th	11.55	00.26	12.06	00.25	1st quarter
15th	12.11	01.42	12.29	01.33	
16th	12.31	03.01	12.55	02.44	
17th	12.56	04.22	13.28	03.58	
18th	13.31	05.43	14.09	05.12	
19th	14.19	07.00	15.01	06.24	
20th	15.25	08.05	16.07	07.28	
21st	16.46	08.55	17.22	08.23	full moon
22nd	18.15	09.32	18.44	09.07	
23rd	19.47	09.59	20.08	09.42	
24th	21.18	10.20	21.29	10.11	
25th	22.45	10.38	22.48	10.37	
26th	–	10.54	–	11.01	
27th	00.09	11.11	00.04	11.24	3rd quarter
28th	01.30	11.28	01.18	11.49	
29th	02.49	11.48	02.28	12.16	
30th	04.03	12.13	03.36	12.48	
31st	05.13	12.45	04.40	13.24	

In the night sky this month

1st	Possible sighting of Comet 46P/Wirtanen from good dark sky sites. Visible from about 19.00 at 45 degrees altitude in the northeastern sky. Reaches 80 degrees in the north at around 00.30 on the 2nd before becoming lost in the northwest dawn at around 06.00. Similarly placed for the next week or so.
2nd	Close approach of Venus and the moon, which rise at about 05.00 in the east and reach 20 degrees above the southeastern horizon, becoming lost in the dawn at 07.30.
3rd & 4th	Quadrantids meteor shower.
12th	Close approach of Mars and the moon, first visible in the dusk at around 17.00 in the south, at their highest altitude of 41 degrees. They set in the west at about 22.30.
21st	Total lunar eclipse. The moon starts to darken at around 03.00. Full eclipse at 05.00, when the moon will be at 26 degrees altitude in the west and appear dark red due to light scattered by the earth's atmosphere. Eclipse ends at around 06.30.
22nd	Close approach of Venus and Jupiter, which rise in the southeast at about 05.00. They reach an altitude of 14 degrees in the south–southeast before becoming lost in the dawn at 07.30.
30th	Close approach of the moon, Venus and Jupiter, which rise at about 05.00 in the east–southeastern sky. They rise to 14 degrees altitude in the southeast before becoming lost in the dawn.

NATURE

Inside the beehive in January

In the depths of winter, the main task for the beehive is keeping warm. There are very few flowers to visit anyway, and the colony stays inside the hive and survives on its stores of precious honey from the previous summer, or sometimes on sugar water provided by the beekeeper. To keep warm, the bees huddle closely together in a football-sized circle that spreads across several frames, called a 'winter cluster'. The centre of the cluster can stay as warm as 38°C even when it is freezing outside. Bees on the outside of the cluster will stay almost motionless in cold weather, but those on the inside can move around a little in all but the coldest weather.

Look out for...fox breeding season

In cities and suburbs on January nights you may hear male foxes fighting, or the unearthly cries of female foxes mating. This is fox breeding season, just a couple of weeks long, and litters of four or five cubs will be born in March. Cubs stay inside the den for six to eight weeks, and will start tentatively venturing out to play, frolic and explore around June or July. They will be fully grown by September and finally leave the family in October to set up their own territories nearby.

NATIVE TREES – WINTER TWIGS

THE GARDEN

Planting by the moon

New moon to 1st quarter: 6th–14th. Sow crops that develop below ground. Dig the soil.

1st quarter to full moon: 14th–21st. Sow crops that develop above ground. Plant seedlings and young plants.

Full moon to 3rd quarter: 21st–27th. Harvest crops for immediate eating. Harvest fruit.

3rd quarter to new moon: 27th–4th February. Prune. Harvest for storage. Fertilise and mulch the soil.

Job of the month – plant a tree

Deepest winter is the perfect time for planting trees. For smaller gardens look at crab apples, paperbark maple (*Acer griseum*) or the broad-leaved hawthorn *Crataegus persimilis* 'Prunifolia'. Plant now and stake well. Keep your new tree well watered all through its first year, after which it should be established enough to fend for itself.

Glut of the month – kale

Handsome green-black cavolo nero, also known as black kale, is one of the few vegetables still looking good on the vegetable plot.

- **Crispy seaweed:** Shred 300g kale, make sure it is completely dry, then deep-fry before sprinkling sugar, salt and Chinese five spice powder over it. Mix and serve.
- **Bubble and squeak:** Form steamed kale and pre-cooked potatoes (boiled or roasted) into cakes and fry in butter until golden on each side. Top with a runny fried egg.
- **Kale and walnut winter pesto:** Blitz 2 handfuls of raw kale (stems removed) with 60g toasted walnuts, 60g grated Parmesan, 150ml extra virgin olive oil, the juice of half a lemon and salt and pepper. Stir into hot pasta.

Flower of the month – snowdrop

Latin name: *Galanthus nivalis* (*Galanthus* from the Greek
gala, meaning 'milk', and *anthos*, meaning 'flower'; *nivalis*
from Latin, meaning 'snowy, snow-covered, snow-like').
Common names: Mary's tapers, dingle-dangle, Candlemas
bell. In France they are called *perce-neige*, which means
snow-piercer.

Post-Christmas winter is the grimmest bit. No more hustle
and bustle, present-giving and nonstop partying. Just the
cold and the dark and the overwhelming feeling that you've
slightly overdone it on several fronts. But step out into your
garden on New Year's Day and there will be a reassuring
sign that winter is moving on, and that spring will come:
snowdrops, poking fresh green through the cold earth, and
soon to produce their delicate, pure white hanging droplets of
flowers. Unsurprisingly, they are symbols of purity, optimism
and hope, and as such are closely associated with Candlemas
on 2nd February, which is the only day they can be brought
into the house without incurring bad luck. Snowdrops will
collapse if frozen, but they quickly perk up again when
temperatures rise, so don't worry: their leaves contain a sort
of 'anti-freeze' that prevents the cells from being damaged
by frost. If you don't have any snowdrops in your garden,
just after flowering is the time to remedy this, by buying and
planting them 'in the green', before the leaves have died down.

THE KITCHEN

Cheese of the month – Gorwydd Caerphilly

Caerphilly is a fairly quick cheese, maturing within two to three months, and although it was originally made in Wales, many Somerset Cheddar makers have also long taken it on because of its quick turnaround. And this is the case with Trethowan's Dairy, in Somerset. There is a distinct difference between the summer and winter batches of their Gorwydd Caerphilly. In summer the cows graze the pastures. The fresh grass takes on water and so the milk has a low fat content. This makes the curds fairly dry, crumbly and acidic, and the creamy layer that forms between the rind and the centre – the 'breakdown' – thin, producing a light, refreshing cheese. From around mid-October the cows are kept in a barn and fed a richer diet of silage and hay. The milk, produced for the winter needs of calves, is more calorific. The winter cheese is softer, plumper and creamier but still with that characteristic brittle Caerphilly texture and lactic flavour. The breakdown is more pronounced, and the flavour towards the mushroomy rind is savoury. Winter cheeses are ready just before Christmas and remain available until May.

In season

Stalwarts like **kale, kohlrabi, leeks, cabbage, cauliflower, carrot** and **swede** are still standing in the garden. Early varieties of **purple sprouting broccoli** start to produce this month.

Well-stored **apples** and **pears, beetroot, carrots, garlic, onions, parsnips** and **squash** are all still good.

This is the high point for imported citrus, and this month **bergamot oranges** and the very first **blood oranges** join in – plus, of course, the prized **Seville oranges**, which you can snap up for marmalade making. There are also lots of imported **pineapples, kiwis, passion fruits** and **pomegranates**.

Black truffles are still arriving from Italy.

Hare, woodcock, pheasant and **venison** are available from some butchers. **Duck** and **goose** are in season until the end of the month.

Cod, whiting, Dover sole, haddock, pollock, bass, scallops, mussels and **oysters** are all in season.

RECIPES

Epiphany tart

There is a long English tradition, dating back to at least the 1600s, of creating tarts topped with intricate pastry patterns and coloured with different jams – the forerunners of the humble jam tart. Although they were originally the preserve of the pastry cooks of the gentry, over time the challenge was taken up by ordinary housewives, particularly in the north of England, for special church occasions. There were many designs, but when made in a star shape it was known as an Epiphany tart and served on 6th January. The star is made from two overlapping triangles (like the Star of David), and this provides 13 'wells' for 13 different jams – one each for Jesus and the 12 disciples.

Ingredients

220g plain flour
Pinch of salt
100g cold butter, diced
Cold water
Jam in up to 13 different flavours

Method

If you have a food processor, blitz together the flour, salt and butter until it resembles breadcrumbs. If doing it by hand, rub the butter into the flour and the salt with your fingertips. Once you have a breadcrumb texture by whichever method, add a little cold water, just a couple of tablespoons at first, and stir it in with your hands before bringing it together into a dough. Add more water if necessary. Knead once or twice, then wrap in clingfilm and refrigerate for 30 minutes.

Preheat your oven to 200°c, Gas Mark 6. Take the pastry from the refrigerator and cut it in half. Roll one half out thinly, then use it to line a 23cm flan tin. Cut the other

half into 6 pieces, and roll each into a sausage, before using
each as one side of the 2 triangles, overlapping the triangles
to form the star shape. Fill the gaps in with spoonfuls of jam.
Bake for 25–30 minutes, or until the pastry is cooked. Cool and
serve in wedges.

Salt-preserved citrus

Citrus is at its cheapest, best and most varied now. Some citrus
varieties flower in late winter and take 12 months to become
mature fruit, while others fruit all year round, but they are
harvested in greater quantity just before the coldest time in
the year. A great number are shipped to the British Isles for
marmalade making and eating: Seville oranges, limes, lemons,
clementines, blood oranges and even – if you're lucky – oddities
such as bergamots. All of these can be very simply preserved in
salt, just as lemons are traditionally, and will make intriguing
and fragrant additions to recipes throughout the year. You will
need 1-litre preserving jars, sterilised.

Ingredients

Rock salt

Citrus fruits

Peppercorns

Cardamom pods

Star anise

Bay leaves

Method

Put a thin layer of rock salt and spices at the base of your jar.
If using small citrus such as lemons, limes or bergamots, slice
each from the top to almost the bottom into 8 pieces, leaving

the bases intact so that they hold together. Open up each fruit and pour 1 tablespoon salt into it, then nestle it into the jar. Larger fruits such as Seville oranges will need to be sliced into segments, and each fruit sprinkled with 1 ½ tablespoons salt. Layer spices in as you go, using a few peppercorns and cardamom pods per jar and a star anise and bay leaf in each. Cram the jars full, pushing the contents down with your fingers or a wooden spoon.

Seal, then shake each jar every day for a couple of weeks – the juices will slowly seep from the fruits to fill the jar. They will be ready after a month, but better after 2 or 3 months.

To use them, take a fruit from the jar and scoop out and discard the flesh. Rinse the skin under the tap to remove some of the saltiness, then chop and add to tagines, herby salads, rice and couscous. Add small pieces to cakes and biscuits in place of candied peel.

Cullen skink

Cullen skink is a traditional thick and creamy smoked haddock soup from the northeast coast of Scotland. This cosy and comforting stomach liner is often eaten as the starter for a Burns Night supper on 25th January, but it is perfect warming fare throughout the winter months.

Serves 6

Ingredients

500g smoked haddock

300ml water

1 bay leaf

100g butter

2 leeks, washed and chopped
2 medium-sized potatoes, peeled and chopped into chunks
500ml whole milk
Salt and pepper
Chives, snipped, to serve

Method

Put the fish, water and bay leaf into a low, wide pan, cover and bring to the boil. As soon as the water boils, take it off the heat. Leave it to sit for a couple of minutes and then lift the fish – which should now be cooked – out onto a plate, reserving the cooking water. When the fish is cool, flake it, discarding any bones and skin.

Melt the butter in a saucepan and then sweat the leeks, covered, for at least 20 minutes, until they are soft and translucent. Add the potatoes and stir well, then add the water and bay leaf from the fish pan. Simmer gently – you may need to add a splash more water but try to resist adding much. Instead, keep the temperature low and steady and stir frequently. When the potatoes are tender, lift out a couple of big spoonfuls of the mixture and set aside. Add the milk and half the fish to the saucepan and bring to a simmer, then blend with a stick blender. Add the rest of the fish, and the reserved leek and potato mixture. Heat through, season with salt and lots of pepper, and serve, topped with snipped chives.

A SONG FOR BURNS NIGHT

'Ae Fond Kiss'
Robert Burns

On Burns Night on 25th January, cullen skink, haggis and tatties followed by cranachan are eaten, and the poems and songs of Robert Burns are recited, to celebrate the life of the great Scottish poet. 'Ae Fond Kiss' is one of his most beautiful songs and was written after his final meeting with his adored friend Mrs Agnes McLehose, known to her friends as Nancy, on her leaving Scotland to attempt a reconciliation with her estranged husband in Jamaica.

Ae fond kiss, and then we sev er! Ae fare -

weel, al - as for - ev er, Deep in heart - wrung tears i'll

pledge thee, War - ing sighs and groans i'll wage thee.

Who shall say that Fortune grieves him,
While the star of hope she leaves him?
Me, nae cheerful twinkle lights me;
Dark despair around benights me.

I'll ne'er blame my partial fancy,
Naething could resist my Nancy;
But to see her was to love her;
Love but her, and love for ever.

Had we never lov'd sae kindly,
Had we never lov'd sae blindly,
Never met – or never parted,
We had ne'er been broken-hearted.

Fare-thee-weel, thou first and fairest!
Fare-thee-weel, thou best and dearest!
Thine be ilka joy and treasure,
Peace, Enjoyment, Love and Pleasure!

Ae fond kiss, and then we sever!
Ae fareweel, alas, for ever!
Deep in heart-wrung tears I'll pledge thee,
Warring sighs and groans I'll wage thee.

February

- **1** Imbolc (pagan celebration)
- **1** St Brigid's/St Bride's Day (Christian/pagan)
- **1** Start of LGBT history month
- **2** Candlemas (Christian)
- **5** Chinese New Year – Year of the Pig begins
- **10** Saraswati Puja/Vasant Panchami (Hindu spring festival)
- **14** St Valentine's Day/Birds' Wedding Day
- **15** Parinirvana Day/Nirvana Day – commemorating Buddha's death and achieving parinirvana (Buddhist)

The naming of February

> Gearran (Scots Gaelic)
> Februar (Scots/Ulster Scots)
> Feabhra (Irish Gaelic)
> Toshiaght-arree (Manx)
> Chwefror (Welsh)
> Hwevrer (Cornish)
> Févri (Jèrriais)

At first glance it seems as if the languages of the British Isles have very little agreement over the naming of February, but, in fact, most of them have origins in the Latin name for the month, *Februarius*, which in itself arises from *februum*, meaning 'purification' (this is often the month of Lent and fasting, though not this year). If you say the Welsh Chwefror and the Cornish Hwevrer aloud, the similarities become clearer. However, the Scots Gaelic Gearran takes a different route this month – *gear an* means 'short month', which, of course, this is. Manx, likewise, goes its own way, as *toshiaght* means 'start' or 'beginning', and *arree* means 'spring' which is a hopeful and optimistic thought.

A CHINESE NEW YEAR STORY FOR FEBRUARY

The great race

The Jade Emperor – the gentle and caring ruler of the gods in Chinese mythology – asked all of the animals to gather for a race to celebrate his birthday. The first 12 animals would be given a place as his guards at the heavenly gate for ever more, and so all of the animals were keen to do their best.

The race was across a great wide river, and the quick-witted rat noticed the ox, steady and dependable, and leapt upon his ear as he started to swim the river. The ox didn't notice, and carried the rat over. The rat leapt from his ear and crossed the finish line first, but the ox, being kind-natured, happily took second place. Next came the tiger, surging confidently out of the water, followed by the rabbit, who had skilfully hopped upon a log and drifted across. The good-natured dragon was next, having slowed down when he had noticed the rabbit on the log, and having used his breath to sweep the rabbit across. Clever snake and lively horse came next, followed by the shy goat and the clever monkey, the courageous rooster and the loyal dog. Finally, puffing over the water, came the generous and easy-going pig. He had become hungry and stopped to eat but had then fallen asleep. The emperor chuckled and announced the race concluded.

Each animal in turn – combined with an element – rules the character of the year, and new-born babies will take on the characteristics of their year's animal. This year Chinese New Year falls on 5th February, and the year of the earth pig begins. Children born this year will be communicative and popular. For everyone else the earth pig signals a lively, joyous and festive year, but grounded and kept from being too frivolous by the earth element.

WEATHER

Winter rainbows

To spot a rainbow, all you need is sunshine and showers, your back to the sun and the rainstorm ahead of you. The effect is created when thousands of raindrops refract white light into the full spectrum. Bold, bright, colourful rainbows mean big raindrops. They can be easier to spot in autumn, winter and spring because of the angle of the sun: the lower the sun is to the horizon, the more of the rainbow we see, and there is no possibility of a sighting once the sun is above 42 degrees above the horizon. High summer suns towards the middle of the day bring arcs so shallow they are lost along or below the horizon, while low winter suns (or morning or evening suns in summer) bring dramatically arched arcs.

Average temperatures (°c):	Inverness 5, Padstow 6
Average sunshine hours per day:	Inverness 3, Padstow 3
Average days of rainfall:	Inverness 17, Padstow 22
Average rainfall total (mm):	Inverness 40, Padstow 78

Day length

During the course of February, day length increases by:

2 hours 7 minutes (to 10 hours 31 minutes) – Inverness

1 hour 36 minutes (to 10 hours 52 minutes) – Padstow

Sunrise and set

	Inverness		Padstow	
	Rise	Set	Rise	Set
1st	08.18	16.42	07.55	17.11
2nd	08.16	16.45	07.53	17.13
3rd	08.14	16.47	07.52	17.15
4th	08.12	16.49	07.50	17.17
5th	08.10	16.52	07.49	17.18
6th	08.08	16.54	07.47	17.20
7th	08.05	16.56	07.46	17.22
8th	08.03	16.59	07.44	17.24
9th	08.01	17.01	07.42	17.25
10th	07.59	17.03	07.41	17.27
11th	07.56	17.06	07.39	17.29
12th	07.54	17.08	07.37	17.31
13th	07.52	17.10	07.35	17.32
14th	07.49	17.13	07.33	17.34
15th	07.47	17.15	07.32	17.36
16th	07.44	17.18	07.30	17.38
17th	07.42	17.20	07.28	17.39
18th	07.39	17.22	07.26	17.41
19th	07.37	17.24	07.24	17.43
20th	07.34	17.27	07.22	17.45
21st	07.32	17.29	07.20	17.46
22nd	07.29	17.31	07.18	17.48
23rd	07.27	17.34	07.16	17.50
24th	07.24	17.36	07.14	17.52
25th	07.22	17.38	07.12	17.53
26th	07.19	17.41	07.10	17.55
27th	07.16	17.43	07.08	17.57
28th	07.14	17.45	07.06	17.58

THE SEA

Average sea temperature

Isle of Lewis:	7.9°C
Whitby:	6.9°C
Belfast:	8.1°C
Cork:	9.5°C
Swansea:	8.5°C
Brighton:	8.7°C
Falmouth:	10°C

Spring and neap tides
The spring tides are the most extreme tides of the month, with the highest rises and falls, and the neap tides are the least extreme, with the smallest. Exact timings vary around the coast, but expect them around the following dates:

Spring tides: 7th–8th and 20th–21st

Neap tides: 13th–14th and 27th–28th

In the tide timetable opposite, spring tides are shown with an asterisk.

February tide timetable for Dover

For your local high tide differences on Dover, see page 8.

	High water		Low water	
	Morning	Afternoon	Morning	Afternoon
1st	08.54	21.22	03.20	15.54
2nd	09.49	22.08	04.27	16.53
3rd	10.32	22.47	05.20	17.39
4th	11.07	23.22	06.02	18.16
5th	11.39	23.55	06.37	18.48
6th	–	12.10	07.08	19.18
7th	00.26	12.39	07.38	19.48 *
8th	00.53	13.04	08.09	20.19 *
9th	01.16	13.28	08.41	20.51
10th	01.42	13.57	09.13	21.23
11th	02.16	14.33	09.46	21.59
12th	02.57	15.19	10.24	22.41
13th	03.48	16.18	11.13	23.38
14th	04.56	17.52	–	12.23
15th	06.37	19.30	01.02	13.54
16th	07.57	20.35	02.30	15.10
17th	09.00	21.31	03.41	16.18
18th	09.55	22.21	04.47	17.24
19th	10.45	23.08	05.50	18.25
20th	11.31	23.53	06.48	19.17 *
21st	–	12.15	07.39	20.03*
22nd	00.36	12.58	08.24	20.42
23rd	01.19	13.41	09.04	21.17
24th	02.03	14.25	09.41	21.53
25th	02.48	15.12	10.18	22.30
26th	03.36	16.05	10.59	23.14
27th	04.31	17.08	11.50	–
28th	05.38	18.23	00.15	12.56

THE SKY AT NIGHT

Moon phases

New moon – 4th February

1st quarter – 12th February

Full moon – 19th February

3rd quarter – 26th February

In the night sky this month

10th	Close approach of Mars and the moon, first visible in the dusk at around 17.30 in the south, at 43 degree altitude. They set in the west at about 23.00.
27th	Close approach of the moon and Jupiter, which rise at around 03.00 in the southeastern sky. They rise to 15 degrees in the south before becoming lost in the dawn at 06.30.

Moon rise and set

	Inverness		Padstow		
	Rise	Set	Rise	Set	
1st	06.15	13.25	05.39	14.07	
2nd	07.07	14.15	06.30	14.57	
3rd	07.48	15.13	07.14	15.53	
4th	08.20	16.18	07.50	16.53	new moon
5th	08.45	17.27	08.21	17.55	
6th	09.05	18.38	08.47	18.59	
7th	09.21	19.49	09.10	20.04	
8th	09.35	21.01	09.30	21.09	
9th	09.49	22.13	09.50	22.14	
10th	10.02	23.27	10.10	23.21	
11th	10.17	–	10.32	–	
12th	10.34	00.43	10.56	00.29	1st quarter
13th	10.56	02.00	11.24	01.40	
14th	11.24	03.19	12.00	02.51	
15th	12.04	04.36	12.45	04.02	
16th	12.59	05.45	13.42	05.08	
17th	14.11	06.41	14.51	06.06	
18th	15.36	07.24	16.10	06.55	
19th	17.09	07.56	17.34	07.35	full moon
20th	18.43	08.21	18.59	08.07	
21st	20.15	08.40	20.22	08.36	
22nd	21.44	08.58	21.42	09.01	
23rd	23.10	09.15	23.00	09.25	
24th	–	09.32	–	09.50	
25th	00.32	09.52	00.15	10.17	
26th	01.51	10.15	01.26	10.48	3rd quarter
27th	03.04	10.45	02.33	11.23	
28th	04.09	11.22	03.34	12.04	

THE GARDEN

Planting by the moon

New moon to 1st quarter: 4th–12th. Sow crops that develop below ground. Dig the soil.

1st quarter to full moon: 12th–19th. Sow crops that develop above ground. Plant seedlings and young plants.

Full moon to 3rd quarter: 19th–26th. Harvest crops for immediate eating. Harvest fruit.

3rd quarter to new moon: 26th–6th March. Prune. Harvest for storage. Fertilise and mulch the soil.

Job of the month – plant bulbs 'in the green'

Bulbs from moist woodland habitats such as snowdrops, winter aconites and bluebells can struggle if treated like normal bulbs – that is, dried out, stored dry and replanted in autumn. Instead, they should be planted while still in active growth and just after flowering, and for snowdrops and winter aconites that means now. Look for specialist nurseries that offer them in this state, for happier bulbs and more flowers.

Glut of the month – Oriental greens

If you sowed mizuna, mibuna, pak choi and giant red mustard last August, you will now have healthy and colourful leaves to pick.

- **Sea bass with mizuna:** Take a sheet of foil and lay a handful of mizuna leaves under a portion of sea bass or haddock, then top with soy sauce, lime juice, chopped ginger and chopped chilli. Close the parcel, leaving space for steam, and bake at 190°C, Gas Mark 5 for 20 minutes.
- **Pak choi and udon noodles:** Poach pak choi and stir into a miso broth with udon noodles, topped with a poached egg.
- **Winter salad:** Make a spicy winter salad of mibuna leaves with julienned carrot and apple. Dress with lime and extra virgin olive oil, and top with toasted and crushed peanuts.

Flower of the month – sweet violet

Latin name: *Viola odorata* (*Viola* from the Latin for the colour violet; *odorata* from the Latin for 'sweet smelling').
Common names: sweet violet, wood violet, English violet, florist's violet, lesbian flower.

We will be told plenty of times this month that violets are blue, when they are clearly violet: just like orange, the colour was named after the thing. They are in flower this month, very much unlike roses (which are often red), but sadly they are rarely given as Valentines despite the fact that they have traditionally been understood to be a romantic token, meaning 'My thoughts are occupied with love' in the Victorian language of flowers. They are particularly associated with lesbian love and were known in 1920s New York as the 'lesbian flower', possibly because of a poem by Sappho in which she describes herself and her lover wearing violets: 'If you forget me, think of our gifts to Aphrodite and all the loveliness that we shared, all the violet tiaras, braided rosebuds, dill and crocus twined around your young neck.'

There are other violets around but you can identify sweet violet by its strong perfumed scent. They make a wonderful and medicinal syrup, if you can gather enough. Home is in damp and semi-shady spots, peeking out from under hedgerows and spread across woodland floors, but they are also easy to cultivate in similar spots in gardens. Track down seed from specialist suppliers, and sow some future love tokens of your own now.

THE KITCHEN

Cheese of the month – Sleightlett

Mary Holbrook's goats roam around Sleight Farm in Somerset, eating weeds and wildflowers and whatever they come across. They are also managed naturally, allowed to stop lactating in autumn (some goat farmers use artificial lighting to trick goats into breeding in winter so that they keep producing milk). In January they start kidding, and so they start to produce milk again, and it's only in February that the year's first rounds of Sleightlett are produced. The milk has a small amount of rennet and a starter added to it, and then there is a long wait, of up to 48 hours, for the curds to form. Mary carefully ladles the curds into the mould and leaves them to drain, then sprinkles them with charcoal ash. This is as young a cheese as you can find; it matures for just three days, after which time it can be eaten immediately – pure white, creamy and lactic – or kept for up to another week and a half only. As the herbs, flowers and grasses on the farm change through spring and summer, the subtle flavours within the cheese change, too, but it is always fresh, delicate and herbal.

In season

There may still be a few **blood oranges** around next month but this is their peak, so get some now. Imported **kiwi fruits**, **passion fruits**, **pineapples** and **pomegranates** are also plentiful and at their best.

Leeks, kale and cabbages are still going well outdoors, if starting to look a little battered, and beautiful **purple sprouting broccoli** is now coming thick and fast.

Black truffles are still available.

Pears, apples, carrots, swede and **parsnips** are still good from storage.

This is the final month of the **venison** season.

Clams, cockles and **muscles** are all in season until March.

RECIPES

Blood orange and pistachio cake

A sunny cake for a gloomy time of year, making use of the fleeting blood orange crop. Catch it while you can (though this recipe will work with navel oranges – or indeed any citrus – the rest of the year). The blood orange juice makes a very pretty pink icing, if you're Valentine-minded.

Ingredients

For the cake

150g butter

150g caster sugar

Zest of 3 blood oranges and juice of 1

2 eggs

150g self-raising flour

1 teaspoon baking powder

160g pistachios, roughly chopped

For the icing

5 tablespoons icing sugar

Juice of half a blood orange

Method

To make the cake, preheat the oven to 190°C, Gas Mark 5, oil a 20cm cake tin and line it with baking parchment. Beat the butter, caster sugar and zest together until light and fluffy, and then add the eggs, one at a time, beating until well combined before adding the next. Pour in the juice and beat it into the mixture, then add the flour, baking powder and 150g of the pistachios, reserving some to sprinkle on top. Gently mix everything until well combined, then tip into the prepared tin and smooth down. Bake in the centre of the oven for around

30–35 minutes, until a cocktail stick poked into the centre meets some resistance and comes out clean. Let the cake cool for 10 minutes in the tin, and then remove it and leave it to cool completely on a wire rack.

To make the icing, sift the icing sugar into a small bowl and add a little of the juice, stirring to make a thick paste, then gradually add the rest of the juice until you have a runny icing. When the cake is completely cool, spread the icing over it, allowing some to drip down the sides. Sprinkle the remaining chopped pistachios over the top.

Sichuan-style bacon, a recipe for Chinese New Year by Li Ling Wang

Among Asian communities it is traditional to hold a lavish feast with friends and family to celebrate the lunar New Year. Every dish on the table has a symbolic significance for the year ahead, and great care and thought are put into choosing dishes that will bring blessings. Meat is particularly important to the feast, and the absence of bacon and sausages on the New Year's table indicates that the work of the past year will bring no gains in the new year.

In China many people cannot often get hold of fresh meat, and rural families will kill a pig two months before Chinese New Year and preserve it as bacon. This feeds the family through winter and makes a delicious and essential dish for the Chinese New Year table. There are regional variations but the basic method is the same; this version is from Sichuan province in southwestern China. Sometimes it is smoked over Cypress branches or peanut shells to further preserve it and add even more flavour.

Ingredients

2kg boneless pork (belly or the fat part of the ribs)
100g salt
2 tablespoons ground Sichuan pepper
50g sugar
200ml soy sauce
2 teaspoons five spice powder
50ml vodka or other flavourless white spirit
100g sweet bean sauce (available in Chinese supermarkets)
2 teaspoons chicken stock powder (optional)

Method

Cut the meat into long strips 5–6cm wide, and pat dry with a clean cloth. Mix the salt and half the Sichuan pepper, then sprinkle evenly over the meat, rubbing it in well. Place in a covered container and put in the refrigerator to marinate for 2 days, turning it over halfway through.

After it has marinated, pour out the saltwater and pat the meat dry with a clean cloth. Return the meat to the container and add the remaining ingredients. Rub them well into the meat and return to the refrigerator for 4 days, turning the meat daily. After this time remove from the container and pat dry with a clean cloth. Thread the pieces with string and then hang them up in a cool, ventilated place for 7 days to dry, being careful not to get the meat wet or to let the pieces touch.

Wash the dried meat slices with hot water, then poach them in boiling water for about 20 minutes. Either eat as they are, or cool and then use with stir-fried vegetables. (You can steam the slices instead of poaching them, but that will make them a bit saltier.)

PIG BREEDS

GLOUCESTER OLD SPOT

OXFORD SANDY AND BLACK

TAMWORTH

SADDLE BACK

BERK SHIRE

NATURE

Inside the beehive in February

February can be very cold, and in these conditions the colony is still using all of its energy to keep warm and stay alive. But there are a few flowers out now, and in mild winters the bees will start to make brief forays to visit snowdrops and crocuses in sunny spots, and to collect some early pollen, before quickly returning to the warmth of the hive. They also use these short early flights to clean themselves after a winter indoors. In mild winters the queen may lay a few eggs in February, to get ahead, but the larvae must be kept warm in the very centre of the cluster.

Look out for...bluetit display flights

Male bluetits start singing heartily in February, impressing potential mates that they have made it through winter and with energy to spare. If you are lucky you may also spot one making odd display flights, which is all part of the show: he will utter a brief, trembling trill before setting off in a parachuting glide towards a female's chosen nest site, or he might beat his wings shallowly and rapidly, moving between nearby perches. Despite the bravado, this is a tough time for these birds. They will have been weakened by winter, and natural food sources are now very low as winter drags on. Putting out high-fat foods such as sunflower seeds, peanuts in net bags, grated suet or fat balls can help them make it through cold nights. Clean, non-frozen water is a life-saver now, too.

A SONG FOR VALENTINE'S DAY

'Tomorrow is St Valentine's Day'
William Shakespeare

This bawdy tale of love, lust and very swift rejection serves as a warning to maids not to come to bed too readily, Valentine's Day or no. It is sung by Ophelia in *Hamlet*, after he rejects her, but is thought likely to be an older song that would have been well known to Shakespeare's audiences.

The young man rose and donned his clothes,
And dupped the chamber door,
Let in the maid that out, a maid,
Never departed more.

Quoth she, Before you tumbled me,
You promised me to wed,
That would I have done, by yonder sun,
If thou hadst not come to my bed.

By Gis and by Saint Charity,
Away and fie for shame.
Young men will do it, when they come to it,
By cock, they are to blame.

March

- **1** Start of meteorological spring
- **1** St David's Day – patron saint of Wales
- **5** St Piran's Day – patron saint of Cornwall (and tin miners)
- **5** Shrove Tuesday – pancake day
- **6** Ash Wednesday, beginning of Lent (Christian)
- **11** Commonwealth Day
- **17** St Patrick's Day – patron saint of Ireland
- **18** St Patrick's Day bank holiday, Northern Ireland and Republic of Ireland
- **20** Vernal equinox, start of astronomical spring
- **20** Ostara (pagan celebration of spring)
- **20** 20th–21st: Holi (Hindu spring festival)
- **21** Nowruz (Iranian/Persian New Year)
- **25** Lady Day, The Feast of the Annunciation (Christian)
- **31** Fourth Sunday in Lent – Mothering Sunday (Christian)
- **31** British Summer Time begins. Clocks go forward one hour at 01.00

The naming of March

> Màrt (Scots Gaelic)
> Mairch (Scots/Ulster Scots)
> Márta (Irish Gaelic)
> Mayrnt (Manx)
> Mawrth (Welsh)
> Meurth (Cornish)
> Mar (Jèrriais)

This month there is universal agreement between the languages of the British Isles. All hark back to *Martius*, the first month of the Roman calendar, which itself comes from Mars, the Roman god of war and of agriculture, this being his month. March's position as the first month of the year was widespread, and 25th March was considered the first day of the year in England until 1752.

AN IRISH CATHOLIC TALE FOR MARCH

The story of St Patrick

St Patrick started life as Maewyn Succat, a boy from a rich family living an easy life in Roman Britain in the 5th century, somewhere near Cumbria. But when he was about 16 years old the path of his life dramatically changed: Irish pirates raiding his family's estate captured him and carried away across the Irish Sea, where he was enslaved and forced to herd and tend sheep.

Ireland was at that time ruled by many kings and by a priestly caste of druids, who worshipped an ancient race of heroic fighting and feasting gods called the Tuatha Dé Danann. It was a loose, earthy and hedonistic religion, its stories passed by word of mouth. Maewyn used his time in the fields devoutly praying and finding a faith in God, as well as observing the Irish way of life and learning the Irish language. After six years of captivity he fled from his master and sailed home, where he studied Christianity.

Acting on a vision, he returned as a Christian missionary to Ireland, where he used his understanding of the Irish culture to convert people from their old pagan ways; famously, he used the shamrock to illustrate the Holy Trinity. He came into conflict with the druid priests and Irish kings, and even apocryphally met with and attempted to convert the very god-warriors themselves. Despite having no luck in that respect, he went on to successfully convert and baptise thousands of Irish people, and is credited with bringing Christianity to Ireland. Hailed as the 'Apostle of Ireland', he referred to himself in writings as Patricius, which means 'father of the citizens'.

Patrick is thought to have died on 17th March, and this became his feast day. Over time he has become particularly associated with Catholic Ireland, with the colour green – which in the Irish flag represents Catholics – and with Irish national identity. Wherever the Irish diaspora has settled in large numbers around the world, St Patrick's Day is a day to gather, drink, sing and celebrate all things Irish.

WEATHER

March winds

Wind is the result of a difference in air pressure between two neighbouring areas. The more extreme the difference, and the closer the two areas, the greater the wind. High air pressure tends to come with cold air and low pressure with warm. In March the sea around the British Isles is still extremely cold, but the land is being heated by an increasingly warm sun, leading to great differentials. At the same time the jet stream starts to head northwards, which brings warm weather while driving areas of low pressure towards us. It is a time of considerable instability and turbulence before warmth wins out later in spring. Air rushes to equalise the pressure, resulting in high winds.

Average temperatures (°C):	Inverness 6, Padstow 7
Average sunshine hours per day:	Inverness 4, Padstow 4
Average days of rainfall:	Inverness 19, Padstow 22
Average rainfall total (mm):	Inverness 40, Padstow 68

Day length

During the course of March, day length increases by:

2 hours 28 minutes (to 13 hours 4 minutes) – Inverness
1 hour 54 minutes (to 12 hours 50 minutes) – Padstow

The vernal equinox is on Wednesday, 20th March, at 21.58. The sun will reach an altitude of 38 degrees at midday.

Sunrise and set

| | Inverness | | Padstow | |
	Rise	Set	Rise	Set
1st	07.11	17.47	07.04	18.00
2nd	07.09	17.50	07.02	18.02
3rd	07.06	17.52	07.00	18.04
4th	07.03	17.54	06.58	18.05
5th	07.01	17.57	06.56	18.07
6th	06.58	17.59	06.53	18.09
7th	06.55	18.01	06.51	18.10
8th	06.52	18.03	06.49	18.12
9th	06.50	18.05	06.47	18.14
10th	06.47	18.08	06.45	18.15
11th	06.44	18.10	06.43	18.17
12th	06.42	18.12	06.40	18.19
13th	06.39	18.14	06.38	18.20
14th	06.36	18.17	06.36	18.22
15th	06.33	18.19	06.34	18.24
16th	06.31	18.21	06.32	18.25
17th	06.28	18.23	06.30	18.27
18th	06.25	18.25	06.27	18.28
19th	06.22	18.28	06.25	18.30
20th	06.19	18.30	06.23	18.23
21st	06.17	18.32	06.21	18.33
22nd	06.14	18.34	06.18	18.35
23rd	06.11	18.36	06.16	18.37
24th	06.08	18.38	06.14	18.38
25th	06.06	18.41	06.12	18.40
26th	06.03	18.43	06.10	18.41
27th	06.00	18.45	06.07	18.43
28th	05.57	18.47	06.05	18.45
29th	05.55	18.49	06.03	18.46
30th	05.52	18.51	06.01	18.48
31st	06.49	19.54	06.59	19.49

British Summer Time starts on 31st March at 01.00, and this is accounted for above.

THE SEA

Average sea temperature

Isle of Lewis:	7.6°C
Whitby:	6.8°C
Belfast:	8.0°C
Cork:	9.4°C
Swansea:	8.3°C
Brighton:	8.2°C
Falmouth:	9.7°C

Spring and neap tides

The spring tides are the most extreme tides of the month, with the highest rises and falls, and the neap tides are the least extreme, with the smallest. Exact timings vary around the coast, but expect them around the following dates:

Spring tides: 8th–9th and 22nd–23rd

Neap tides: 15th–16th and 29th–30th

In the tide timetable opposite, spring tides are shown with an asterisk.

March tide timetable for Dover

For your local high tide differences on Dover, see page 8.

	High water		Low water	
	Morning	Afternoon	Morning	Afternoon
1st	07.04	19.49	01.30	14.08
2nd	08.39	21.00	02.47	15.20
3rd	09.38	21.49	04.00	16.25
4th	10.19	22.27	04.58	17.16
5th	10.50	23.01	05.41	17.55
6th	11.17	23.31	06.16	18.27
7th	11.45	23.59	06.47	18.57
8th	–	12.12	07.17	19.28 *
9th	00.24	12.37	07.48	19.58 *
10th	00.49	13.01	08.19	20.29
11th	01.15	13.30	08.49	21.00
12th	01.48	14.06	09.20	21.33
13th	02.28	14.50	09.55	22.14
14th	03.16	15.46	10.41	23.08
15th	04.21	17.16	11.46	–
16th	06.20	19.13	00.28	13.25
17th	07.48	20.23	02.05	14.50
18th	08.53	21.20	03.22	16.04
19th	09.48	22.10	04.33	17.13
20th	10.37	22.56	05.39	18.11
21st	11.20	23.38	06.35	19.00
22nd	–	12.01	07.23	19.43 *
23rd	00.19	12.40	08.04	20.19 *
24th	01.00	13.19	08.41	20.53
25th	01.40	14.00	09.15	21.25
26th	02.21	14.43	09.48	21.59
27th	03.06	15.33	10.23	22.36
28th	03.59	16.32	11.07	23.31
29th	05.03	17.42	–	12.14
30th	06.21	19.05	00.54	13.34
31st	09.09	21.26	03.14	15.46

British Summer Time starts on 31st March at 01.00, and this is accounted for above.

THE SKY AT NIGHT

Moon phases

New moon – 6th March

1st quarter – 14th March

Full moon – 21st March

3rd quarter – 28th March

In the night sky this month

11th	Close approach of Mars and the moon, first visible in the dusk at around 18.30 in the south, at 41 degrees altitude. They set in the west at about 23.00.
27th	Close approach of the moon and Jupiter, which rise at around 02.00 in the southeastern sky. They rise to 16 degrees in the south before becoming lost in the dawn at 05.30.

Moon rise and set

	Inverness		Padstow		
	Rise	Set	Rise	Set	
1st	05.05	12.09	04.27	12.52	
2nd	05.49	13.05	05.13	13.46	
3rd	06.24	14.09	05.52	14.45	
4th	06.50	15.17	06.24	15.47	
5th	07.11	16.27	06.51	16.51	
6th	07.28	17.39	07.15	17.55	new moon
7th	07.43	18.51	07.36	19.01	
8th	07.56	20.30	07.56	20.06	
9th	08.10	21.17	08.16	21.13	
10th	08.24	22.32	08.36	22.21	
11th	08.39	23.49	08.59	23.30	
12th	08.59	–	09.25	–	
13th	09.24	01.06	09.57	00.40	
14th	09.58	02.22	10.37	01.49	1st quarter
15th	10.44	03.32	11.27	02.55	
16th	11.47	04.32	12.29	03.55	
17th	13.04	05.19	13.41	04.46	
18th	14.31	05.54	15.01	05.28	
19th	16.04	06.21	16.25	06.03	
20th	17.37	06.42	17.49	06.32	
21st	19.09	07.00	19.12	06.59	full moon
22nd	20.39	07.17	20.33	07.24	
23rd	22.06	07.34	21.52	07.48	
24th	23.30	07.53	23.08	08.15	
25th	–	08.15	–	08.45	
26th	00.48	08.42	00.19	09.19	
27th	01.59	09.17	01.24	09.59	
28th	03.00	10.01	02.22	10.45	3rd quarter
29th	03.49	10.55	03.12	11.38	
30th	04.27	11.57	03.53	12.36	
31st	05.56	14.04	05.27	14.37	

British Summer Time starts on 31st March at 01.00, and this is
accounted for above.

Meteor shower of the month – the Virginids

Several minor meteor showers make up the Virginid Meteor
Complex, which pulses through January to May, mostly
peaking in March and April. It is thought possible that all
of these small meteor showers may be caused by the fiery
burning up of debris from the same comet – D/1766 G1 –
but that this space dust has been pulled apart over time into
several distinct clouds by the gravitational fields of the eight
planets. D/1766 G1 was independently identified by several
astronomers when it passed by earth in April 1766, visible
to the naked eye and with a tail 3–4 degrees long. This is no
spectacular show – perhaps one or two meteors per hour – but
if you see a meteor at this time of year it is likely to belong to
one of the Virginids showers.

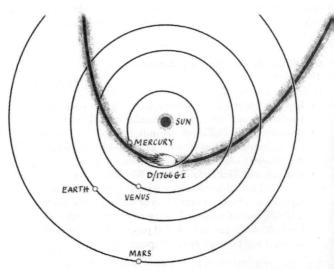

THE GARDEN

Planting by the moon

New moon to 1st quarter: 6th–14th. Sow crops that develop below ground. Dig the soil.

1st quarter to full moon: 14th–21st. Sow crops that develop above ground. Plant seedlings and young plants.

Full moon to 3rd quarter: 21st–28th. Harvest crops for immediate eating. Harvest fruit.

3rd quarter to new moon: 28th–5th April. Prune. Harvest for storage. Fertilise and mulch the soil.

Job of the month – pot up chrysanthemums

This is the time to get your cutting garden under way. Pot chrysanthemum cuttings up somewhere frost-free, ready to be planted out when frosts have passed. They will need to be protected from slugs when they first go out. If you have nowhere that you can keep them frost-free, then hold on and buy plants later in the season, when the weather is warm enough for them to go out.

Glut of the month – purple sprouting broccoli

This spring treat is at its height this month, pumping out endless spears and admirably filling the 'hungry gap'.

- **Broccoli frittata:** Put steamed spears, crunchy pieces of fried bacon and some grated Cheddar into a big frittata.
- **Broccoli, garlic, chilli and almonds:** Boil the broccoli for 2 minutes, drain, then fry with garlic and chilli before topping with toasted slivered almonds.
- **Broccoli with Hollandaise sauce:** Whisk together 2 egg yolks, 1 tablespoon lemon juice, 1 teaspoon Dijon mustard in a bowl set over a pan of boiling water. Slowly add 100g melted butter, whisking as you go. Finish with a splash of vinegar and salt and pepper, then serve with steamed and buttered broccoli spears.

Flower of the month – daffodil

Latin name: *Narcissus* (named after the mythological character, Narcissus).
Common names: daffadowndilly, narcissus, jonquil, Easter lily, Lent lily.

Narcissus was the beautiful and vain hunter who, stumbling across a still pool, fell in love with his own reflection and wasted away, gazing at himself. Daffodils were given the name *Narcissus* because of their downward nodding habit, but it seems unfair that these jolly, bold, straightforward flowers have been saddled to such a nincompoop. If anything, their movement is far more like overenthusiastic waving than it is self-involved navel-gazing.

The daffodil has become the second emblem of St David's Day, which falls on 1st March, the first being the leek, as St David advised the Britons to wear leeks in their caps so they could tell friend from foe in battle. The Welsh for leek is *cenhinen* while the Welsh for daffodil is *cenhinen Pedr*, and so confusion between the two is one possible explanation for the dual emblems. Victorian sensibilities are another possibility: pinning a leek to your coat was felt a little uncouth and so pretty daffs were substituted. Wales has its very own daffodil in the form of the diminutive and bright yellow Tenby daffodil, *Narcissus obvallaris*, which mainly grows in South Wales.

Daffodils are among the simplest of flowers to grow, the only tricks being getting their bulbs in the ground good and early in autumn, and letting the leaves die down of their own accord after flowering.

DAFFODILS

M

NATURE

Inside the beehive in March

As the weather warms and the days lengthen, activity within the hive increases. Lots of worker bees – non-reproducing female bees that do most of the work of the hive – must be raised to replace the bees that have died over winter, and so the queen starts laying lots of eggs into brood cells which are situated in the centre of the frame and capped with a small dome of yellowy wax. There are more forays out of the hive to gather from early bloomers – wood anemone, sweet violets, blackthorn, pussy willow and goat willow – and hopefully return with pollen baskets laden. This month is essential to replenish the hive's stores after the long winter: a wet and cold spring with few flowers can be disastrous, but a mild spell now will set the colony up for a bumper summer.

Look out for...hedgehogs coming out of hibernation

Hedgehogs emerge from hibernation this month, hungry, thirsty and disorientated: they will have lost a third of their body weight over winter and need to replenish it fast, ready for breeding season. Make a hedgehog feeding station so that they can eat and drink away from predators such as foxes and badgers. Cut a 12–15cm square hole in one end of a large plastic storage box with a lid, covering the sharp edges with duct tape. Place newspaper in the box, and then place a bowl each of water and a meat-based cat food (chicken is best – no fish) at the end farthest from the hole. Tuck the box under a hedge or into a border. Put a weight such as a brick on the lid so it doesn't come off. You can make a feeding station even if you have never seen a hedgehog in your garden: they are hard to spot even if they are there, and are also in extreme decline, so worth taking a punt on.

THE KITCHEN

Cheese of the month – Hafod

The best cheese preserves the qualities of the milk it was made with, and so March's batch of Hafod cheddar – which takes 9–10 months to mature – is captured summer pasture. By last May and June, the Ayrshire herd at Bwlchwernen Fawr, Wales' oldest organic dairy farm, would have been outside day and night, and so getting the food they love best and that makes the best milk: a herbal ley of clover, timothy, chicory and meadow fescue by day and permanent pasture meadows at night. The milk is unpasteurised, to retain its broad bandwidth of flavours, and long-lost gentle and slow Cheddar-making techniques from the early 20th century use a light touch to turn it into cheese. The cheese, which was wrapped in cloth and covered in lard, has matured over winter. Every batch has subtle differences, and March's cheese has brighter, toppier, grassier flavours, reflecting the diet of the herd at the time it was made.

In season

The first stirrings of new growth mean that **Swiss chard, spring onions** and **winter lettuces** are ready for harvesting now. On woodland floors **wild garlic** has emerged and is ready to be picked. The last of the **Brussels sprouts** can be picked. There is plenty of **purple sprouting broccoli** and **rhubarb**. **Winter cabbages** are on their way out but **spring cabbages** are beginning.

This is the last month for stored **cooking apples**. Stored **eating apples** and **pears** are over.

Oysters and **mussels** are still in season but will soon be gone. **Halibut, cod, coley, dab, lemon sole** and other winter fish are still in season too.

RECIPES

Welsh leek rarebit

Welsh rarebit was once known as Welsh rabbit, when 'Welsh' was used in a derogatory way to imply a substitute for the real thing (for instance, to use a 'Welsh comb' meant to comb your hair with your fingers). The name 'rarebit' is thought to have come along later as a way of making the dish sound fancy. Fancy it isn't, but cheesy, savoury and quick it is. You can make the rarebit ahead of time and keep it in the refrigerator for up to a week, ready to spread and toast any time.

Serves 4
Ingredients
50g salted butter
1 leek, halved and washed, then finely sliced
225g strong Cheddar cheese, grated
2 teaspoons Worcestershire sauce
1 level teaspoon mustard powder
1 level tablespoon flour
4 tablespoons beer
4 slices of bread

Method
Melt the butter in a pan and add the leeks; stir them in and cover the pan. Let them sweat for at least 10 minutes, stirring occasionally, until they are collapsed and silky. Add the cheese, Worcestershire sauce, mustard and flour; stir together, then add the beer and heat gently until everything is combined into a thick paste. You will need to leave it to cool for 10 minutes before you use it.

Toast the bread on one side. Spread the rarebit evenly over the untoasted side of each slice of bread. Grill until bubbly and eat as soon you can without burning the roof of your mouth.

M

Fridge-pickled rainbow chard

The colourful stems of rainbow chard make a beautiful jewel-coloured pickle, and if you quick-pickle them they don't have time to lose their colour to the pickling solution. The leafy part and stem part of chard have different cooking times anyway, so remove the greens and steam or stir-fry them for a separate dish. This pickle will be ready after 24 hours, and will keep for several weeks in the refrigerator.

Ingredients
About 20 rainbow chard stems, green parts removed
300ml white wine vinegar
2 tablespoons salt
2 tablespoons caster sugar
½ teaspoon black peppercorns
½ teaspoon mustard seed
A few whole allspice
1 bay leaf

Method
Wash and trim the chard stems then cut them into 5cm lengths. Place them in a jar or a plastic container that has a tight-fitting lid. Gently heat all of the other ingredients together until the sugar and salt have dissolved, then bring to the boil and simmer for a few minutes before pouring over the stems. Seal and leave to cool, then store in the refrigerator, turning the stems occasionally to make sure all have a turn in the pickling liquor. They are ready to use after 24 hours.

A SONG FOR ST PATRICK'S DAY

'Paddy's Green Shamrock Shore'
Traditional

Many Irish folk songs are about leaving Ireland and then
longing for it, sometimes by enforced transportation at the
hands of the harsh British penal system, sometimes economic
emigration across the Atlantic to escape poverty and famine.
This song is in the latter tradition, but is one of the more jolly
examples: everyone arrives safe and excited to seek their fortune.
If it weren't for the longing for sweet Liza and those shamrock-
coloured shores this could almost count as a happy ending.

So fare thee well, sweet Liza dear and likewise Derry town
And twice farewell to my comrade boys that dwell on that
    sainted ground
If fortune it should favour me, and I to have money in store
I'll come back and I'll wed the wee lassie I left on Paddy's green
shamrock shore.

At twelve o'clock we came in sight of famous Mullin Head
And Innistrochlin to the right stood out on the ocean's bed.
A grander sight ne'er met my eyes than e'er I saw before
Than the sun going down 'twixt sea and sky far away from the
    shamrock shore.

We sailed three weeks, we were all seasick, not a man on board
    was free
We were all confined unto our bunks and no-one to pity poor
    me.
No father kind nor mother dear to lift up my head, which was
    sore
Which made me think more on the lassie I left on Paddy's green
    shamrock shore.

We safely reached the other side after fifteen and twenty days,
We were taken as passengers by a man and led round in six
    different ways,
We each of us drank a parting glass, in case we'd meet no more
And we drank a health to old Ireland and Paddy's green
    shamrock shore.

April

1   April Fools' Day

3   Isra and Mi'raj – The Miraculous Night Journey (Muslim)

8   Vesak – Buddha Day (Buddhist)

14   Vaisakhi (Sikh and Hindu celebration of the solar new year)

14   Rama Navami (Hindu celebration of the god Rama)

14   Palm Sunday (Christian)

19   Good Friday, (Christian) holiday

20   Passover/Pesach (Jewish) – festivities begin at sundown on the 19th

21   Easter Day (Christian)

22   Easter Monday, (Christian) holiday, England, Wales and Northern Ireland

23   St George's Day – patron saint of England

23   Shakespeare Day

26   Orthodox Good Friday

28   Orthodox Easter Sunday

29   Orthodox Easter Monday

The naming of April

> Giblean (Scots Gaelic)
> Apryle (Scots/Ulster Scots)
> Aibreán (Irish Gaelic)
> Averil (Manx)
> Ebrill (Welsh)
> Ebryll (Cornish)
> Avri (Jèrriais)

The *Fasti Praenestini* is an ancient Roman calendar carved in marble, or at least the remains of it. Only parts of January, March, April and December survive, but it has left a tantalising clue as to the origins of the name of this month. The Roman month *Aprilis* is derived from *aperio*, 'to open', and the *Fasti* has an idea as to why: 'Fruits and flowers and animals and lands and seas do open' this month, it says. Most of the names for April in the languages of the British Isles appear to have originated with *Aprilis*, with the possible exceptions of the Irish Gaelic Aibreán and the Scots Gaelic Giblean, which may come from *braon*, meaning 'drops of rain'.

A JEWISH TALE FOR APRIL

The Passover Seder

The Israelites were the slaves of ancient Egypt, and the people from whom modern Jews believe they are descended. They were subjected to cruelty and hard labour and forced to build the pyramids and to work in the fields. Moses went to the Pharaoh and asked him to set his people free, but the Pharaoh refused, so God rained ten plagues down upon Egypt. The first nine – in which water turned to blood, the Nile teemed with frogs, lice crawled over men and beasts, wild animals attacked, livestock were diseased, festering boils afflicted men and animals, hail fell, locusts swarmed, and three days of darkness spread over Egypt – failed to move the Pharaoh; the Israelites remained enslaved. Finally, God told the Israelites to sacrifice a lamb and to daub the blood on their doorways. He sent an angel of death to kill all of the first-born children in the land, but to pass over those with the blood mark. Overnight, every Egyptian first-born in the land was killed. The Pharaoh set the Israelites free and commanded them to leave immediately.

The evening of 19th April this year brings the start of Passover, or Pesach, and the first Seder, which commemorates the exodus from Egypt of the Israelites. It is part ritualised meal, part retelling of the story, which Jews are obliged to repeat each year: it is thought that the Last Supper may have been a Passover Seder. Jews use a book known as the Haggadah, which means 'the telling', to guide them through the evening.

The Seder Plate is central to the telling. It contains six traditional items: Maror and Chazeret (bitter herbs, such as parsley or endives), for the bitter times the Israelites had endured; Zeroa (the shank bone of a lamb), for the sacrificial Paschal Lamb; Beitzah (an egg), for hope; Charoset (a paste of apples, nuts and wine), for the mortar the Israelites were forced to use to build ancient Egypt; and Karpas (parsley or a green vegetable), which is dipped in salted water and represents the Israelites' hard labour and tears. Matzah (unleavened bread) accompanies these six items, symbolising the fact that the Israelites had to leave so quickly that their bread did not have time to rise.

WEATHER

Final frost dates

The date of the last frost is impossible to predict accurately, but it is possible to make some rough guesses that can be useful when determining if it is safe to put your pelargoniums out yet. The Scillies and the Channel Islands barely get any at all. On the mainland the south coast is frost free earliest in the year, where the combination of the sea's ameliorating influence and simply being south can see it frost-free from 1st March. Southern cities such as Bristol, Portsmouth and London are next in line, benefiting from the heat-island effect and proximity to water, and along with a few areas of the west coast of Scotland and the east coast of northern Ireland, warmed by the Gulf Stream, they can hope to be frost-free from around 10th March. The rest of the coast and a few northern cities (Manchester, Glasgow) plus the west coast of Ireland are looking at being frost-free from around 10th April. The vast majority of inland Britain and the middle and east coast of Ireland are slightly later, around the end of April. Frost lingers longest in the Highlands of Scotland where it can arrive into June. Treat these guidelines with caution and always check local weather forecasts before casting any clouts.

Average temperatures (°C):	Inverness 7, Padstow 9
Average sunshine hours per day:	Inverness 5, Padstow 6
Average days of rainfall:	Inverness 18, Padstow 20
Average rainfall total (mm):	Inverness 30, Padstow 64

Day length

During the course of April, day length increases by:

2 hours 20 minutes (to 15 hours 29 minutes) – Inverness
2 hours 46 minutes (to 14 hours 40 minutes) – Padstow

Sunrise and set

	Inverness		Padstow	
	Rise	Set	Rise	Set
1st	06.46	19.56	06.56	19.51
2nd	06.43	19.58	06.54	19.53
3rd	06.41	20.00	06.52	19.54
4th	06.38	20.02	06.50	19.56
5th	06.35	20.05	06.48	19.58
6th	06.32	20.07	06.45	19.59
7th	06.30	20.09	06.43	20.01
8th	06.27	20.11	06.41	20.02
9th	06.24	20.13	06.39	20.04
10th	06.22	20.15	06.37	20.06
11th	06.19	20.18	06.35	20.07
12th	06.16	20.20	06.33	20.09
13th	06.13	20.22	06.30	20.10
14th	06.11	20.24	06.28	20.12
15th	06.08	20.26	06.26	20.14
16th	06.05	20.29	06.24	20.15
17th	06.03	20.31	06.22	20.17
18th	06.00	20.33	06.20	20.18
19th	05.58	20.35	06.18	20.20
20th	05.55	20.37	06.16	20.22
21st	05.52	20.39	06.14	20.23
22nd	05.50	20.42	06.12	20.25
23rd	05.47	20.44	06.10	20.26
24th	05.45	20.46	06.08	20.28
25th	05.42	20.48	06.06	20.30
26th	05.40	20.50	06.04	20.31
27th	05.37	20.53	06.02	20.33
28th	05.35	20.55	06.00	20.34
29th	05.32	20.57	05.58	20.36
30th	05.30	20.59	05.57	20.37

A

THE SEA

Average sea temperature

Isle of Lewis:	8.3°C
Whitby:	8.1°C
Belfast:	8.8°C
Cork:	10.2°C
Swansea:	9.6°C
Brighton:	9.6°C
Falmouth:	10.6°C

Spring and neap tides

The spring tides are the most extreme tides of the month, with the highest rises and falls, and the neap tides are the least extreme, with the smallest. Exact timings vary around the coast, but expect them around the following dates:

Spring tides: 8th–9th and 20th–21st

Neap tides: 13th–14th and 27th–28th

In the tide timetable opposite, spring tides are shown with an asterisk.

April tide timetable for Dover

For your local high tide differences on Dover, see page 8.

	High water		*Low water*	
	Morning	Afternoon	Morning	Afternoon
1st	10.12	22.19	04.25	17.49
2nd	10.52	22.58	05.23	18.41
3rd	11.20	23.30	06.08	18.23
4th	11.47	–	06.45	18.58
5th	00.00	12.14	07.18	19.30
6th	00.28	12.42	07.51	20.03
7th	00.54	13.08	08.24	20.36
8th	01.21	13.36	08.56	21.08 *
9th	01.51	14.08	09.27	21.40 *
10th	02.26	14.46	09.59	22.15
11th	03.07	15.33	10.36	22.57
12th	03.58	16.33	11.23	23.53
13th	05.10	17.13	–	12.28
14th	07.13	19.54	01.14	14.08
15th	08.36	21.05	02.48	15.33
16th	09.40	22.03	04.05	16.46
17th	10.34	22.53	05.17	17.53
18th	11.21	23.37	06.21	18.49
19th	12.03	–	07.15	19.36
20th	00.19	12.41	08.01	20.17 *
21st	00.59	13.19	08.41	20.54 *
22nd	01.38	13.58	09.16	21.27
23rd	02.18	14.37	09.48	21.59
24th	02.58	15.19	10.18	22.30
25th	03.41	16.06	10.48	23.03
26th	04.31	17.01	11.23	23.49
27th	05.32	18.05	–	12.22
28th	06.42	19.17	01.11	13.52
29th	08.04	20.33	02.33	15.05
30th	09.20	21.32	03.40	16.06

THE SKY AT NIGHT

Moon phases

New moon – 5th April

1st quarter – 12th April

Full moon – 19th April

3rd quarter – 26th April

In the night sky this month

9th	Close approach of Mars and the moon, first visible in the dusk at around 19.30 in the west, at an altitude of 32 degrees. They set in the northwestern sky at about 00.30.
23rd	Close approach of the moon and Jupiter, which rise at around midnight in the southeastern sky. They rise to 16 degrees in the south before becoming lost in the dawn at 05.00.
25th	Close approach of the moon, Saturn and Jupiter. They rise at around 03.00 over the southern horizon and reach about 15 degrees altitude before becoming lost in the dawn.
26th	Close approach of the moon and Saturn, which rise at 02.00 over the southeastern horizon. They reach an altitude of 15 degrees before becoming lost in the dawn at 05.00.

Moon rise and set

	Inverness		Padstow		
	Rise	Set	Rise	Set	
1st	06.18	15.14	05.56	15.40	
2nd	06.36	16.26	06.20	16.45	
3rd	06.51	17.38	06.42	17.50	
4th	07.04	18.51	07.02	18.56	
5th	07.17	20.06	07.21	20.04	new moon
6th	07.31	21.21	07.41	21.12	
7th	07.46	22.39	08.03	22.22	
8th	08.03	23.57	08.28	23.33	
9th	08.26	–	08.58	–	
10th	08.57	01.14	09.35	00.43	
11th	09.38	02.26	10.21	01.50	
12th	10.34	03.29	11.18	02.51	1st quarter
13th	11.45	04.18	12.25	03.43	
14th	13.06	04.56	13.40	04.27	
15th	14.34	05.24	15.00	05.02	
16th	16.05	05.46	16.21	05.32	
17th	17.35	06.04	17.43	05.59	
18th	19.05	06.20	19.04	06.23	
19th	20.34	06.36	20.24	06.47	full moon
20th	22.01	06.54	21.43	07.12	
21st	23.25	07.14	22.58	07.40	
22nd	–	07.38	–	08.12	
23rd	00.42	08.10	00.09	08.50	
24th	01.50	08.51	01.12	09.35	
25th	02.45	09.42	02.06	10.26	
26th	03.28	10.42	02.52	11.23	3rd quarter
27th	04.00	11.48	03.29	12.24	
28th	04.24	12.58	03.59	13.27	
29th	04.43	14.09	04.25	14.32	
30th	04.59	15.22	04.47	15.37	

A

Meteor shower of the month – the Lyrids

At the end of April the earth's orbit takes it through the dust particles left behind by Comet Thatcher (C/1861 G1), which passed us in 1861 before setting off on its own 415-year orbit around the sun. The shower runs from 16th to 25th April but peaks in intensity on the night and early morning of the 22nd and 23rd, when you can hope to see up to 20 meteors per hour: look out for persistent trains, ionised gas trails that glow for a few seconds after the meteor has appeared, seen in about a quarter of Lyrid meteors. Some years it produces bursts of up to 100 meteors per hour, but this is unpredictable. Unfortunately, this year the peak comes just a few days after the full moon, so viewing conditions are not ideal.

NATURE

Inside the beehive in April

The brood of new worker-bee larvae must be kept warm no matter how cold it becomes outside, and 'nurse' bees may dip into the last of the winter honey stores from the wax-capped cells along the top of the frame to produce body heat. When these crucial first worker bees of the year chew their way out of their cells, they go straight to work visiting wild cherry blossom, cowslips, dandelions, clover and the first apple blossom and bluebells, and starting the year's work. But honey making is not the main task just yet. First they collect nectar for energy (stored in glistening open cells just below the capped winter honey) and pollen for protein (creating multicoloured and multi-textured cells as varied as the flowers they have visited, just below the pollen cells) to feed and fuel the fast-expanding colony.

Look out for...brimstone butterflies

The first butterflies of the year are very often brimstone butterflies, the females palest green and the males butter yellow. It is thought that the word butterfly is derived from 'butter-coloured fly' after the male of this species. They are so early because they hibernate through winter as adults in outbuildings, cracks in stone walls and hollows in trees rather than overwintering as pupae. This is so that they can emerge as soon as the weather warms, though it can leave them vulnerable to early emergence during mild spells, or to late cold snaps. Brimstone is another word for sulphur, the colour of the wings.

THE GARDEN

Planting by the moon

New moon to 1st quarter: 5th–12th. Sow crops that develop below ground. Dig the soil.

1st quarter to full moon: 12th–19th. Sow crops that develop above ground. Plant seedlings and young plants.

Full moon to 3rd quarter: 19th–26th. Harvest crops for immediate eating. Harvest fruit.

3rd quarter to new moon: 26th–4th May. Prune. Harvest for storage. Fertilise and mulch the soil.

Job of the month – sow tender annuals

Early April is the moment to get all of your tender annual seeds underway (or mid-April if you live in a cold area). Tender flowers such as sunflowers, zinnias, cosmos, nicotiana, tithonia and cleomes, and fruits and vegetables such as tomatoes, cucumbers, melons, aubergines, courgettes, French beans, runner beans and sweetcorn can be sown in a greenhouse or on sunny windowsills, to be planted out about six weeks later, after the last frosts.

Glut of the month – parsley

Parsley holds on well over winter, producing fresh growth during mild spells. As the days lengthen it can run to flower and seed and then need ripping out, so use it with abundance now.

- **Salsa verde:** Whizz or chop together 2 big handfuls of parsley with 1 clove crushed garlic, a little fresh mint and basil if you have it, 1 tablespoon capers, 1 gherkin, 6 anchovy fillets, a little Dijon mustard, a splash of vinegar and lots of extra virgin olive oil. Dollop onto chops and sausages.
- **Parsley tempura:** Make a batter using equal parts flour and cold sparkling water, plus a sprinkle of salt, then dip sprigs of parsley in it before frying them in a pan of hot oil. Drain on kitchen paper and eat immediately.

- **Tabbouleh:** Make parsley the star of the show by roughly chopping several handfuls of parsley plus a little fresh mint, then mix in some cooked bulgur wheat, chopped tomatoes, chopped cucumber and chopped spring onions. Dress with lemon juice and olive oil, and serve.

A

Flower of the month – bluebell

Latin name: *Hyacinthoides non-scripta* (*Hyacinthoides* from the Latin, meaning 'like a hyacinth'; *non-scripta*, which is Latin for 'not written'. This relates to the mythical hyacinth of Greek legend created from the blood of dying Hyacinthus and written on in tears by his lover Apollo. So the *non-scripta* part of the name is a way of saying 'and it's not that hyacinth either'.
Common names: English bluebell, wild hyacinth, fairy flower, bell bottle, wood bell.

Bluebell woods produce one of the great natural spectacles of the British Isles this month and next. Exact timing depends on where you are and how cold it has been, but start planning yourself a woodland walk. This is the woodland floor grabbing its moment in the brief period between winter ending and the canopy filling out and blocking light: a temporal niche filled with a sea of purple-blue. The most stunning shows will be under the canopies that cast the densest summer shade, as this suppresses competing ground cover and lets the bluebells dominate. Bluebells are indicator species for ancient woodland, so their presence suggests that a wood dates back to at least 1600.

You can buy bulbs from a reputable supplier in autumn – it is illegal to lift them from the ground – but do consider if your efforts will really rival the sight of a bluebell wood in full purple haze, or if this one is best left to nature.

THE KITCHEN

Cheese of the month – Westcombe ricotta

Cheese is made by first curdling milk to separate the milk
solids (the curds) from the liquid (the whey). The curds are
packed into moulds and treated in various ways to make
different cheeses, but the whey is usually considered a waste
product and at best is fed to pigs, at worst poured away. In the
spring and summer months at Westcombe Cheddar makers,
when the milk is flowing, this makes for a lot of waste, and so
Westcombe, located in Somerset, have started to make like the
Italians and reboil their whey to make ricotta (which literally
means 'recooked'). By adding an acid and heating the whey,
any milk solids left in the liquid are extracted, and they are
then ladled into moulds to settle and drain before being ready
to eat immediately. The best ricotta is made from the best milk,
which comes in now as the cows go out into the fields. Ricotta
is hugely useful in cooking: in cakes, pastries and puddings as
well as in savoury dishes and particularly as a fresh, creamy,
lemony base for a pasta sauce.

In season

The first early **radishes** are starting, and the very first few spears
of **asparagus** are poking their heads out of the ground. **Rocket,
sorrel, spring onions, watercress** and wild **nettles** can be found,
and the last of the **purple sprouting broccoli**.

Jersey Royals arrive in the greengrocers early this month.
There is still plenty of **rhubarb** to be had.

Halibut, crab and **salmon** are now coming in, and **shrimp,
whitebait** and **lobster** are in season.

Spring lamb is available, with the first meat coming from
the southwest of the country. Tender and succulent, it is
particularly mild in flavour.

RECIPES

Twice-baked ricotta with garlic, sea salt, herbs and lemon (and the first asparagus spears)

This dish makes the most of ricotta's ability to absorb flavours, and the trick to making it the most delicious it can be is to douse it repeatedly in the herb-infused oil as it cooks. Ricotta from a deli is firmer than that from the supermarket, but if you can't get the real thing, beat an egg into your supermarket ricotta to help it firm up on baking.

A

Serves 4 as a lunch or more as a snack

Ingredients

500g ricotta (ideally from a cheesemonger or deli)

6 tablespoons extra virgin olive oil

4 garlic cloves, thinly sliced

A few bay leaves

2 sprigs rosemary, needles stripped and roughly chopped

Large handful of thyme stems, roughly chopped

Large handful of oregano stems, roughly chopped

½ teaspoon sea salt

2 bunches asparagus spears, ends trimmed off

Juice of half a lemon

Method

Preheat the oven to 200°C, Gas Mark 6. Oil and line a 450g loaf tin with baking parchment. Tip in the ricotta and smooth it out, then bake for 20 minutes. Leave to cool and firm up for 30 minutes.

Pour half the olive oil into a large roasting tray, and scatter the garlic around the centre, topped with half the herbs, to make a 'bed' for the ricotta. The bed should be twice the width of your ricotta loaf. Tip the cooled ricotta out of the tin, lay it on a board and slice it horizontally through the middle, then place each half cut side up on the herbs. Sprinkle the salt and the rest of the herbs over the ricotta, and pour on the rest of the olive oil.

Bake for 30–40 minutes, basting the top with the garlicky, herby oil every 10 minutes or so. After 20 minutes, place the asparagus spears around the cheese, rolling them in the oil, then return the roasting tray to the oven. When the cheese is golden with crispy edges, remove from the oven and squeeze the lemon juice over everything. Allow to cool almost to room temperature, then serve with hunks of bread.

**Jewish chicken soup with kneidlach,
a recipe by Josephine Haller**

After the story of the Passover Seder (see page 75) has been
told on the evening of Passover, there is a lavish Passover meal.
Classic Jewish chicken soup with kneidlach is often the starter.
Kneidlach are dumplings made from matzo meal, the unleavened
crackers that are central to the celebration, but ground up into
a flour. The perfect kneidel is a matter of great debate: some
people like their kneidlach hard, whereas others think soft is
perfection. The kneidlach in this recipe are light and fluffy.

(see page 75)

Serves 12
Ingredients
For the soup
1 chicken, cut into pieces (or 8 chicken thighs)
3 onions
4 litres water
5 carrots, thickly sliced
5 celery sticks, thickly sliced
1 parsnip, halved
3 garlic cloves (optional)
3 tablespoons roughly chopped parsley
3 tablespoons roughly chopped dill
salt and pepper
For the kneidlach
2 eggs lightly beaten
3 tablespoons vegetable oil
1 pinch of chicken stock granules or ¾ teaspoon salt
95g medium matzo meal

Method

Put the chicken pieces in a very large pan. Keeping them whole, pierce the onions with a knife. Add to the pan with the water, carrots, celery, parsnip, garlic (if using), parsley and half the dill. Cover the pan and bring to the boil, then lower the heat to a simmer. Skim and discard the scum that rises to the surface. Season with salt and pepper, and then simmer for 2½ hours, keeping the pan covered.

To make the kneidlach, in a large bowl lightly beat the eggs and the oil. Add the chicken stock granules or salt to the matzo meal, then fold the matzo meal into the egg-and-oil mixture. Cover and chill for 30 minutes. Bring a pan of water to the boil and have a bowl of cold water next to the hob. Dip a tablespoon into the cold water and then take a spoonful of the matzo batter. With wet hands, roll it into a ball, then slip it into the boiling water and reduce the heat so that the water just simmers. Continue with the remaining matzo batter, working relatively quickly, then cover the pan and cook for 15–20 minutes. Remove the kneidlach from the pan with a slotted spoon and transfer to a plate for about 20 minutes to allow them to firm up.

To serve, reheat the soup, adding the remaining dill. Place a few kneidlach in each bowl and pour only the hot broth over them, leaving the spent chicken and vegetables in the pan.

EUROPEAN EASTER BREADS

PASKA
~SLOVAKIA

COLOMBA
~ITALY

PRIMORSKI
USKRSNE BEBE
~CROATIA

TSOUREKI
~GREECE

HOT
CROSS
BUNS
~ENGLAND

A

A SONG FOR SPRING

'When Spring Comes In'
Traditional

This song is a simple and joyful celebration of this lovely moment in the year, when winter is finally relinquishing its grip.

When spring comes in the birds do sing the lambs do skip and

bells do ring, While we en-joy their glor - ious charm so

no-ble and so gay oh the prim-rose blooms and the cow slip too

vi-olets in their sweet re-tire, the ro - ses shi - ning through the briar and

daff-o-downdillies that we ad-mire will die and fade a - way.

Young men and maidens will be seen,
On mountains high and meadows green,
They will talk of love and sport and play,
While these young lambs do skip away.
At night they homeward wend their way,
When evening stars appear.

A

Chorus:
Oh the primrose blooms and the cowslip too,
The violets in their sweet retire, the roses shining through
    the briar,
And the daffadowndillies that we admire will die and fade
    away.

The dairymaid to milking goes, her blooming cheeks as red as
    a rose,
She carries her pail all on her arm so cheerful and so gay,
She milks, she sings, and the valleys ring,
The small birds on the branches there sit listening to this lovely
    fair.
For she is her master's trust and care, she is the ploughman's
    joy.

Chorus

May

1   May Day/Beltane/International Workers' Day

1   Yom Hashoah – Holocaust Memorial Day (Jewish)

5   Start of Ramadan (after sunset, at the sighting of the young crescent moon, Muslim)

6   Early May bank holiday, England, Wales, Scotland, Northern Ireland and Republic of Ireland

9   Liberation Day, local bank holiday Guernsey and Jersey

21   21st–25th: RHS Chelsea Flower Show, London

26   Rogation Sunday, beating the bounds (Christian)

27   Spring bank holiday, England, Wales, Scotland, Northern Ireland

31   Laylat al Qadr – the Night of Power (Muslim)

The naming of May

> Cèitean (Scots Gaelic)
> Mey (Scots/Ulster Scots)
> Bealtaine (Irish Gaelic)
> Boaldyn/Toshiaght souree (Manx)
> Mai (Welsh)
> Me (Cornish)
> Mai (Jèrriais)

There are several distinct origins of the names used for this month around the British Isles. Several – just like 'May' – are clearly derived from the ancient Roman month name *Maius*, named either after Maia, the goddess of spring and fertility, or after the word for elders, *maiores*, as suggested by Ovid. But Irish Gaelic Bealtaine and Manx Boaldyn are derived from Beltane (or Beltaine), the Gaelic May Day festival held on 1st May, roughly halfway between the spring equinox and the summer solstice. It was one of the four Gaelic festivals that mark out the seasons (along with Imbolc, Lughnasadh and Samhain). Beltane was a fire festival and the fires lit that day were thought to have magical and protective qualities – the name Beltane may come from Celtic *belo-tenia* meaning 'bright fire'. Beltane marks the start of summer, and the day that cattle were driven out to summer pastures; a common ritual was to drive them between two fires to protect them from disease.

Cèitean in Scots Gaelic means 'beginning', and a second name for May in Manx is Toshiaght Souree, *toshiaght* meaning 'beginning' and *souree* meaning 'summer'. May marks the start of the months of growth.

A TRADITIONAL ENGLISH STORY FOR MAY

Jack-in-the-green

Jack-in-the-green is nine feet tall, a dome of early summer foliage, beribboned and topped with a crown of flowers. On May Day in towns and cities throughout England he is woken from his slumber, and once awake he dances through the streets accompanied by chimney sweeps and by his attendants, the bogies: green-clad men and women who play music, dance around him and dab green on the noses of curious children. Once Jack has completed his procession, he is slain, to release the spirit of summer.

This strange tradition began in the 17th century in London, as a working-class celebration of trades and of a day off. Milk maids – who were probably continuing earlier Beltane traditions of the gathering at dawn of spring flowers, and the music and dancing – decorated their pails on May Day with silver cups, flowers and ribbons and then went from house to house wearing them on their heads and dancing for pennies.

May Day was also 'Chimney Sweeps' Day', and the sweeps started competing with the milk maids. The result was ever-bigger displays of foliage, flowers and silver to encourage tips, until the foliage covered them completely, and the tradition of Jack-in-the-green was born.

This spread through the towns and cities of the south of England, but by the late 1800s it was strongly disapproved of and given almost entirely negative press, as its raucous, noisy, working-class fun clashed with Victorian sensibilities. It eventually died out in favour of more genteel May Day traditions.

The growing interest in Morris dancing in the 1970s and the Labour government's introduction of the May Day bank holiday combined to spark a revival, and Jack-in-the-green is now seen in many towns and cities. The revival has morphed the tradition back into something more pagan and mystical, bringing at least a little of its original bawdiness, along with a welcome celebration of the rebirth and renewal of early summer.

M

WEATHER

May dew

Tradition says that if you wash your face in the dew before sunrise on 1st May, you will have a flawless complexion all year. Young women used to stay out all night in woods and meadows on May Day eve to catch it at dawn (though there is some suspicion that this might also have served as an excuse to get up to other things). Dew forms on blades of grass when the air is at 'dew point': saturated until any further cooling will result in water condensing into droplets. In spring the ground is still holding on to the cold of winter, chilling the blades of grass that rise from it, and when the moisture-filled air meets the cold blades of grass, water clings. Autumn is also a dewy time of year, but with the ground still heated after the summer, the dew is more likely to form on objects that are away from the ground but are chilled by cold night air, such as spider webs strung between branches.

Average temperatures (°C):	Inverness 7, Padstow 11
Average sunshine hours per day:	Inverness 6, Padstow 7
Average days of rainfall:	Inverness 18, Padstow 19
Average rainfall total (mm):	Inverness 40, Padstow 62

Day length

During the course of May, day length increases by:

2 hours 4 minutes (to 17 hours 30 minutes) – Inverness
1 hour 23 minutes (to 16 hours 7 minutes) – Padstow

Sunrise and set

	Inverness		*Padstow*	
	Rise	Set	Rise	Set
1st	05.27	21.01	05.55	20.39
2nd	05.25	21.03	05.53	20.41
3rd	05.22	21.06	05.51	20.42
4th	05.20	21.08	05.49	20.44
5th	05.18	21.10	05.48	20.45
6th	05.15	21.12	05.46	20.47
7th	05.13	21.14	05.44	20.48
8th	05.11	21.16	05.43	20.50
9th	05.09	21.18	05.41	20.51
10th	05.07	21.21	05.39	20.53
11th	05.04	21.23	05.38	20.54
12th	05.02	21.25	05.36	20.56
13th	05.00	21.27	05.35	20.57
14th	04.58	21.29	05.33	20.59
15th	04.56	21.31	05.32	21.00
16th	04.54	21.33	05.30	21.02
17th	04.52	21.35	05.29	21.03
18th	04.50	21.37	05.28	21.05
19th	04.48	21.39	05.26	21.06
20th	04.46	21.41	05.25	21.07
21st	04.45	21.43	05.24	21.09
22nd	04.43	21.44	05.23	21.10
23rd	04.41	21.46	05.22	21.11
24th	04.40	21.48	05.20	21.13
25th	04.38	21.50	05.19	21.14
26th	04.36	21.52	05.18	21.15
27th	04.35	21.53	05.17	21.16
28th	04.33	21.55	05.16	21.17
29th	04.32	21.57	05.15	21.19
30th	04.31	21.58	05.15	21.20
31st	04.29	22.00	05.14	21.21

M

THE SEA

Average sea temperature

Isle of Lewis:	9.4°C
Whitby:	9.8°C
Belfast:	10°C
Cork:	11.7°C
Swansea:	11.3°C
Brighton:	11.4°C
Falmouth:	11.9°C

Spring and neap tides

The spring tides are the most extreme tides of the month, with the highest rises and falls, and the neap tides are the least extreme, with the smallest. Exact timings vary around the coast, but expect them around the following dates:

Spring tides: 6th–7th and 19th–20th

Neap tides: 13th–14th and 27th–28th

In the tide timetable opposite, spring tides are shown with an asterisk.

May tide timetable for Dover

For your local high tide differences on Dover, see page 8.

	High water		Low water	
	Morning	Afternoon	Morning	Afternoon
1st	10.04	22.15	04.35	16.57
2nd	10.37	23.49	05.22	17.42
3rd	11.08	23.21	06.04	18.22
4th	11.40	23.53	06.44	19.00
5th	–	12.11	07.22	19.37
6th	00.24	12.42	07.59	20.14 *
7th	00.57	13.16	08.35	20.50 *
8th	01.32	13.54	09.09	21.25
9th	02.12	14.37	09.45	22.05
10th	02.59	15.29	10.26	22.51
11th	03.56	16.36	11.16	23.50
12th	05.17	18.01	–	12.24
13th	06.56	19.27	01.09	13.53
14th	08.16	20.40	02.32	15.11
15th	09.20	21.39	03.43	16.20
16th	10.14	22.30	04.52	17.24
17th	11.00	23.16	04.56	18.21
18th	11.42	23.59	06.50	19.09
19th	–	12.21	07.36	19.51 *
20th	00.40	12.59	08.15	20.29 *
21st	01.19	13.38	08.50	21.04
22nd	01.59	14.18	09.23	21.36
23rd	02.38	14.59	09.52	22.06
24th	03.20	15.42	10.19	22.38
25th	04.06	16.31	10.51	23.19
26th	05.01	17.26	11.37	–
27th	06.03	18.29	00.19	12.47
28th	07.10	19.34	01.37	14.09
29th	08.14	20.34	02.46	15.14
30th	09.07	21.22	03.43	16.09
31st	09.50	22.03	04.34	16.58

M

THE SKY AT NIGHT

Moon phases

New moon – 4th May	
1st quarter – 12th May	
Full moon – 18th May	
3rd quarter – 26th May	

In the night sky this month

7th	Close approach of Mars and the moon, first visible in the dusk at around 21.00 in the west, at 23 degrees altitude. They set in the northwestern sky at about 23.30.
21st	Close approach of the moon and Jupiter, which rise before midnight in the southeastern sky. They rise to 16 degrees in the south at 02.30 before becoming lost in the dawn at 04.30 in the southwest.
23rd	Close approach of the moon and Saturn, which rise at 00.30 over the southeastern horizon. They reach an altitude of 17 degrees before becoming lost in the dawn at 04.00.

Moon rise and set

	Inverness		Padstow		
	Rise	Set	Rise	Set	
1st	05.12	16.35	05.07	16.43	
2nd	05.25	17.49	05.27	17.50	
3rd	05.38	19.05	05.46	18.58	
4th	05.52	20.23	06.07	20.09	new moon
5th	06.09	21.43	06.31	21.21	
6th	06.29	23.03	06.59	22.33	
7th	06.57	–	07.34	23.43	
8th	07.35	00.19	08.17	–	
9th	08.26	01.26	09.11	00.47	
10th	09.33	02.20	10.15	01.43	
11th	10.51	03.01	11.28	02.29	
12th	12.17	03.31	12.45	03.06	1st quarter
13th	13.44	03.53	14.04	03.37	
14th	15.13	04.11	15.24	04.03	
15th	16.40	04.27	16.43	04.27	
16th	18.06	04.42	18.01	04.50	
17th	19.34	04.58	19.19	05.13	
18th	20.59	05.16	20.36	05.39	full moon
19th	22.20	05.38	21.49	06.08	
20th	23.34	06.05	22.57	06.43	
21st	–	06.41	23.57	07.25	
22nd	00.36	07.28	–	08.13	
23rd	01.25	08.25	00.47	09.09	
24th	02.02	09.30	01.28	10.09	
25th	02.29	10.40	02.01	11.13	
26th	02.50	11.51	02.29	12.17	3rd quarter
27th	03.07	13.03	02.52	13.22	
28th	03.21	14.16	03.13	14.27	
29th	03.33	15.29	03.32	15.33	
30th	03.46	16.44	03.51	16.41	
31st	03.59	18.01	04.11	17.51	

Meteor shower of the month – the Eta Aquarids

This month we pass through the trail of Halley's Comet. Specks of debris left in its wake burn up as they hit our atmosphere. At the peak – the night and morning of the 6th and 7th – they produce up to 30 fast-streaking meteors per hour, some with long-lasting tails. This year the show coincides with a thin crescent moon that sets early, leaving a dark sky for prime pre-dawn viewing time. We pass through the other side of Halley's debris trail in October, resulting in the Orionids meteor shower. Halley's Comet comes around every 74–79 years, and last visited in 1986. It is now almost at its furthest point before it circles back for its next appearance in 2061: the only comet visible to the naked eye that it is possible to see twice in a lifetime.

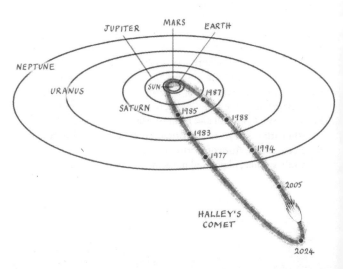

THE KITCHEN

Cheese of the month – garlic yarg

As soon as the wild garlic popped up in March and April, Lynher Dairies cheese makers, based near Truro in Cornwall, were out along the woodland edges gathering up the leaves. Now and into June they will be picking nettle leaves to wrap around their classic Cornish yarg. Both leaves impart distinctive flavours to the young, pale cheese: nettles create a mushroomy rind while the wild garlic leaves infuse the whole cheese with a light garlicky flavour. Yarg is a cows' milk cheese eaten when just six weeks old, and although Lynher Dairies gather enough nettles and wild garlic to freeze and use through the year, the first cheeses using fresh leaves from this year's harvest are ready now. The cheese is creamy under the rind and then slightly more crumbly at the core, with a fresh, milky and lemony flavour. The wild-garlic-wrapped version is moister than the nettle version, simply because the leaves are better at retaining moisture through the maturing process. It is good crumbled over spring salads of young lettuce, broad beans and asparagus.

In season

This is a month for vegetable delicacies from the plot and greengrocer: **asparagus**, **sorrel**, **peas**, **broad beans**, **radish**, **chives** and **chive flowers** and young **spinach**. Tiny **globe artichoke** heads can be picked now: the plant will quickly produce more.

New potatoes are still arriving from Jersey, and are joined by those from Cornwall and from Ayrshire in Scotland.

Rhubarb is still good and British **strawberries** start to reach the greengrocers. **Apricots** arrive from France.

Crab, **sardine**, **plaice** and **mackerel** are all in season.

RECIPES

May wine

May wine (*Maiwein*), sweetened and flavoured with sweet woodruff and early summer fruit, is a German May Day tradition. It is well worth adopting for a May Day celebration, or indeed any outdoor summer event. If possible, gather and dry some sweet woodruff a few days before you need it, as the flavour of dried is much stronger then fresh (You'll find it at the edges of woodland or in hedgerows, and it also makes a good, if vigorous, garden plant for dry shade.)

Serves 10
Ingredients
1 bottle still white wine, chilled
1 good handful sweet woodruff, fresh or dried
Other May herbs and flowers – chamomile flowers, rose petals, lemon verbena
300g strawberries, quartered
1 bottle sparkling white wine, chilled

Method
A few hours before you want it, put the still wine and all the herbs, flowers and strawberries into a big jug, stir and refrigerate. Just before serving, add the sparkling wine, and stir.

Crab and sorrel mayonnaise with rye crackers

Lemony sorrel leaves are up, and are still young and tender enough to be eaten raw. They particularly suit seafood, and crab season has just begun. Homemade crackers and mayonnaise are always worth the trouble, but clearly you can also make this dish a simple assembly job if you buy in both.

Ingredients

1 dressed crab per 2 people

For the crackers

200g rye flour, plus extra for dusting

½ teaspoon baking powder

1 teaspoon sea salt crystals, plus extra for sprinkling

50g cold, salted butter

4 tablespoons cold water

For the mayonnaise

2 egg yolks, at room temperature

½ teaspoon salt

½ teaspoon mustard powder

300ml mild-flavoured oil, such as sunflower or groundnut oil

1 tablespoon lemon juice

2 or 3 young sorrel leaves, cut in thin ribbons

Method

To make the crackers, preheat your oven to 180°C, Gas Mark 4. Mix together the flour, baking powder and salt in a large bowl, then rub in the butter with your fingertips until it resembles breadcrumbs. Add the water and bring the mixture together into a dough using your hands, adding a little more water if necessary. Knead briefly, then roll out on a floured surface until thin – just a few centimetres thick – then cut into rectangular crackers and transfer to a baking tray lined with baking parchment. Prick several times with a fork, brush with water and sprinkle with a few sea salt flakes. Bake for 10-15 minutes or until browned and toasty. Transfer to a wire rack to cool.

To make the mayonnaise, put the egg yolks in a large mixing bowl and beat them for a couple of minutes. Add the salt and mustard powder, and beat for 30 seconds. Begin to add the oil, drop by drop at first, stopping pouring each time to beat it in. As the mixture thickens, you can add a little more at a time, but don't rush or the mayonnaise will separate. Once it has reached the thickness you want (you don't have to add all of the oil), add the lemon juice and mix it in, then the sorrel, and refrigerate until you are ready to use it.

Serve a couple of crackers and a blob of mayonnaise next to the white crab meat (saving the brown crab meat to spread on hot buttered toast).

Apricot, almond and rose-water tarts

In addition to everything else happening at the beginning of May, 3rd May is the feast day of St Philip, the patron saint of pastry chefs.

Makes about 20 tarts

Ingredients

For the pastry

150g plain flour, plus extra for dusting

75g butter

35g icing sugar

1 egg yolk

1 tablespoon cold water

For the filling

100g softened butter

100g caster sugar

½ teaspoon almond extract

½ teaspoon rose-water

Seeds from half a vanilla pod

2 eggs and 1 egg white

100g ground almonds

About 150g apricot jam (1 teaspoon per tart)

3 apricots, each stoned and cut into slices

For the glaze

1 tablespoon apricot jam

1 tablespoon boiling water

Method

To make the pastry, put the flour into a large mixing bowl, then cube the butter and rub it in until it resembles breadcrumbs. Mix in the icing sugar and then the egg yolk and iced water, going in with your hands to bring everything together into a dough. Dust your work surface with flour and thinly roll out the dough. Use an 8cm pastry cutter to cut out about 20 rounds, and fit them into two 12-hole muffin tins or bun tins. Cover with clingfilm and refrigerate for 30 minutes.

To make the filling, cream together the butter, sugar, almond extract, rose-water and vanilla seeds with an electric whisk until creamy and whipped. Add the eggs and egg white, one at a time, whisking to mix each in well before adding the next. Mix in the ground almonds.

To complete the tarts, preheat the oven to 200°C, Gas Mark 6. Take the pastry from the refrigerator and prick the bottom of each round once or twice with a fork. Spoon a teaspoon of apricot jam into each one, and top with the filling. Bake for 10 minutes, then remove the tarts and place a slice of apricot on each and return to the oven. Bake for a further 5–8 minutes, until the filling is well browned. Remove from the oven and, when cool enough, tip out onto a wire rack and leave to cool. Mix together the jam and boiling water and paint the glaze over the fruit and filling.

NATURE

Inside the beehive in May

In arable areas this is boom time, as vast fields of oilseed rape burst into bright yellow flower and the bees go into a frenzy of collection and honey production. Elsewhere they will visit hawthorn, horse chestnut and other spring blossom and flowers. Forager bees collect nectar until their 'honey stomachs' are full, then return to the hive and pass it to the hive bees (also known as receiver bees), which put it into cells near the top of the frame. Nectar is about 80 per cent water and would quickly ferment, so the hive bees beat their wings furiously to evaporate the water content to below 18 per cent. It is then honey and will keep indefinitely, and the bees cap it with wax. If they have space to expand, bees will always make honey as an insurance policy, even when they have plenty in store. Now the beekeeper can take advantage of this and add 'supers' – boxes of frames to be filled with honeycomb – above the main brood box. A 'queen excluder' keeps the queen in the brood box and prevents larvae being laid in the supers. Spring honey may be harvested towards the end of the month, usually pale, light and floral, and set if it contains oilseed rape honey.

Look out for...swallows, swifts and house martins

By late May, swifts are arriving for the summer from their winter home south of the Sahara, swallows from South Africa, and house martins from equatorial Africa. All have predominantly aerial lifestyles and are beautiful to watch in our skies. They are often confused for each other but are easy to tell apart once you know what to look for. Seen from below, a house martin has an entirely white body, with a black head cap, wings and tail tip; the tail has a shallow crescent scoop. A swallow has a white underbody and marking on each wing, and a red head. Its tail is deeply forked with long, elegant tines. Of the three, swifts are the most often seen over cities and suburbs. The swift's body and wings are brown all over and it has a deep scoop shape to its tail; it emits a distinctive, high-pitched, screeching cry.

SWALLOWS, SWIFTS AND HOUSE MARTINS

M

THE GARDEN

Planting by the moon

New moon to 1st quarter: 4th–12th. Sow crops that develop below ground. Dig the soil.

1st quarter to full moon: 12th–18th. Sow crops that develop above ground. Plant seedlings and young plants.

Full moon to 3rd quarter: 18th–26th. Harvest crops for immediate eating. Harvest fruit.

3rd quarter to new moon: 26th–3rd June. Prune. Harvest for storage. Fertilise and mulch the soil.

Job of the month – plant up hanging baskets

Head to the garden centre and buy your bedding plants this month: petunias, lobelias, bedding geraniums and more. You will need around ten small plants for a hanging basket, fewer for a window box: they grow, fill out and bloom quickly as the weather warms. Mix water-retaining gel into the compost to save on watering at the height of summer. In some areas there is still a risk of frost so watch the forecasts and protect your new plantings if needs be.

Glut of the month – peas

If you sowed early, then the first of the year's fresh peas will be ripening now. Eat them within a couple of hours of picking for the sweetest flavour.

- **Peas in their pods:** Boil peas in their pods for a few minutes, drain and serve with a dish of melted butter to dip the whole pod into.
- **Pea salad:** Make a bed of watercress and pile on steamed fresh peas and asparagus topped with ricotta and some torn mint leaves. Dress the lot with lemon juice and extra virgin olive oil, salt and pepper.
- **Pea dip:** Blend cooked peas with feta cheese, olive oil, mint, salt and pepper to make a dip.

Flower of the month – lily of the valley

Latin name: *Convallaria majalis* (*Convallaria* from the Latin *convallis*, meaning 'valley', and *majalis* from the Latin *maius*, meaning 'May').
Common names: May bells, May lily, Our Lady's tears, Mary's tears, ladder-to-heaven, mugget (from the French name for the flower, *muguet*).

M

Fragrant lily of the valley produces its pure white spikes of bell-like flowers in May. It represents chastity, humility and purity, and as such has traditionally been included in wedding bouquets. In the Victorian language of flowers it means, 'You've made my life complete'. Aw. There is a French tradition of giving sprigs of lily of the valley to loved ones on 1st May, which is known as *La Fête du Muguet*, Lily of the Valley Day.

How does it appear from the bare ground? Perhaps it sprang from the earth at the foot of the cross when Mary's tears hit the ground, or from the drops of blood shed by St Leonard as he battled the last dragon in England. Or maybe it is just underground rhizomes that sit tight all winter long, waiting for warmer weather. Lily of the valley is almost too easy to grow, becoming invasive, so plant it in a large area where nothing else will grow. However, it is gorgeous in pots; and you can buy the rhizomes in winter and pot them up indoors to force these beautifully scented flowers to bloom even earlier in the year.

A SONG FOR MAY DAY

'Solidarity Forever'
Ralph Chaplin

1st May is International Workers' Day, more widely known
as May Day, and is often the focus for demonstrations and
marches: a celebration of labourers, workers and the unions
that have helped strengthen their hand and improve working
conditions. 'Solidarity Forever' was written in the US in 1915
by Ralph Chaplin in support of the American union movement
but has been adopted as a union anthem across the world.

Is there aught we hold in common with the greedy parasite,
Who would lash us into serfdom and would crush us with his
    might?
Is there anything left to us but to organise and fight?
For the union makes us strong.

> *Chorus:*
> *Solidarity forever,*
> *Solidarity forever,*
> *Solidarity forever,*
> *For the union makes us strong.*

M

All the world that's owned by idle drones is ours and ours
    alone.
We have laid the wide foundations; built it skyward stone by
    stone.
It is ours, not to slave in, but to master and to own.
While the union makes us strong.

> *Chorus*

They have taken untold millions that they never toiled to earn,
But without our brain and muscle not a single wheel can turn.
We can break their haughty power, gain our freedom when we
    learn
That the union makes us strong.

> *Chorus*

In our hands is placed a power greater than their hoarded gold,
Greater than the might of armies, multiplied a thousand-fold.
We can bring to birth a new world from the ashes of the old
For the union makes us strong.

June

- **1**   Start of meteorological summer
- **1**   Start of Pride Month
- **3**   June bank holiday, the Republic of Ireland
- **4**   4th–5th: Eid al-Fitr – end of Ramadan (Muslim)
- **9**   Feast of Weeks/Shavuot (Jewish) – festivities begin at sundown on 8th
- **9**   Whit Sunday/Pentecost (Christian)
- **16**   Father's Day
- **16**   Trinity Sunday (Christian)
- **20**   Corpus Christi (Christian)
- **21**   Summer solstice, start of astronomical summer – midsommer
- **21**   World Humanist Day
- **24**   Traditional English midsummer, combined with Feast of St John the Baptist (Christian)
- **26**   26th–30th: Glastonbury Festival

The naming of June

> Ògmhios (Scots Gaelic)
> Juin (Scots/Ulster Scots)
> Meitheamh (Irish Gaelic)
> Mean-souree (Manx)
> Mehefin (Welsh)
> Metheven (Cornish)
> Juîn (Jèrriais)

Several of the words used around the British Isles for June are based on the root *haf*, meaning summer: the *hefin* of Welsh Mehefin, the *heven* of Cornish Metheven and the *theimh* of Irish Gaelic Meitheamh. The *me* prefix arises from 'mean' or 'middle', as in the Manx Mean-souree, which means 'middle summer'.

Scots, Ulster Scots and Jersey Jèrriais have derivations of June, from the Latin name for the month, *Junius*, which may be named after either the Roman goddess of marriage, Juno, or the Latin *iuniores*, meaning 'younger ones', or 'juniors'. This could be a counterpoint to May's *maiores*, meaning 'elders'. In keeping with this, the Scots Gaelic Ògmhios means 'young month'.

AN ISLAMIC TALE FOR JUNE

The origins of Ramadan and Eid

Muhammad was a conscientious and idealistic young man, and an orphan. He grew up in Mecca, a mountain town in the high desert plateau of what is now Saudi Arabia, with his grandfather and later his uncle, who took him in after his parents died. When he was a teenager, Muhammad worked as a shepherd to pay his keep, and later as a merchant, marrying at 25 and fathering 6 children. He seemed to be following an expected path, despite his tough start in life. But as he grew older, he grew disillusioned with the world around him, with Mecca's materialism and with his life as a merchant. He sought an answer by visiting a cave in nearby Mount Hira for a month, fasting, meditating and reflecting, then returned the following year, and many years after that.

When he was 40 years old he headed up the mountain once again. He was nearly at the end of his month-long retreat when an angel appeared to him; it was the angel Jibril (Arabic for Gabriel). Jibril said: 'Read!' and presented Muhammad with the first verses of the Quran, telling him that he was destined to be the messenger of Allah, or God. Muhammad was troubled as he descended from Mount Hira, but consultation with his wife and a Christian relative convinced him that he really had been visited by the same angel that had visited Mary before the birth of Jesus. Over the next 23 years, Muhammad returned to the mountain – the Quran was revealed to him and Muhammad became the founding prophet of Islam.

Muslims commemorate Muhammad's month of fasting by themselves fasting from dawn to dusk and dedicating themselves to prayer and contemplation during the Islamic month of Ramadan. This ends when the crescent of the new moon of the next Islamic month, Shawwal, can be seen in the sky, this year on 4th June. Eid al-Fitr – the Festival of the Breaking of the Fast – then commences, a joyful celebration up to three days long. Muslims are released from their religious obligations on Eid al-Fitr, and gather together to feast and offer happy prayers of gratitude to Allah.

WEATHER

The shadow rule

The intensity of UV rays is directly related to the sun's angle above the horizon, and as spring turns to summer the sun rises higher in the sky, where it can do more damage. The shadow rule works all over the world and takes into account altitude, too. If your shadow is shorter than your height, then the sun's rays are strong enough to burn and you need to cover up or seek shade.

Average temperatures (°C):	Inverness 12, Padstow 14
Average sunshine hours per day:	Inverness 6, Padstow 7
Average days of rainfall:	Inverness 19, Padstow 19
Average rainfall total (mm):	Inverness 30, Padstow 70

Day length

During the course of June, day length:

Increases by 28 minutes (to maximum 18 hours 1 minute on 21st), then decreases by 6 minutes by the end of the month – Inverness.

Increases by 19 minutes (to maximum 16 hours 27 minutes on 21st), then decreases by 3 minutes by the end of the month – Padstow.

The summer solstice is on Friday, 21st June, at 16.54. The sun reaches an altitude of 62 degrees at midday. In Inverness, the day of the summer solstice has 11 hours and 26 minutes more daylight than the day of the winter solstice. In Padstow, it has 8 hours and 28 minutes more.

Earliest sunrise: Inverness – 19th June (04.17); Padstow – 17th June (05.07).

Latest sunset: Inverness – 24th June (22.19); Padstow – 25th or 26th June (21.35).

Sunrise and set

| | Inverness | | Padstow | |
	Rise	Set	Rise	Set
1st	04.28	22.01	05.13	21.22
2nd	04.27	22.03	05.12	21.23
3rd	04.26	22.04	05.11	21.24
4th	04.25	22.05	05.11	21.25
5th	04.24	22.07	05.10	21.26
6th	04.23	22.08	05.10	21.27
7th	04.22	22.09	05.09	21.27
8th	04.21	22.10	05.09	21.28
9th	04.21	22.11	05.08	21.29
10th	04.20	22.12	05.08	21.30
11th	04.19	22.13	05.08	21.30
12th	04.19	22.14	05.07	21.31
13th	04.18	22.15	05.07	21.32
14th	04.18	22.16	05.07	21.32
15th	04.18	22.16	05.07	21.32
16th	04.17	22.17	05.07	21.33
17th	04.17	22.17	05.07	21.33
18th	04.17	22.18	05.07	21.34
19th	04.17	22.18	05.07	21.34
20th	04.17	22.19	05.07	21.35
21st	04.17	22.19	05.07	21.35
22nd	04.18	22.19	05.07	21.35
23rd	04.18	22.19	05.08	21.35
24th	04.18	22.19	05.08	21.35
25th	04.19	22.19	05.08	21.35
26th	04.19	22.19	05.09	21.35
27th	04.20	22.19	05.09	21.35
28th	04.20	22.18	05.10	21.35
29th	04.21	22.18	05.10	21.35
30th	04.22	22.18	05.11	21.35

J

THE SEA

Average sea temperature

Isle of Lewis:	11°C
Whitby:	12.7°C
Belfast:	11.8°C
Cork:	13.5°C
Swansea:	13.6°C
Brighton:	13.6°C
Falmouth:	14.1°C

Spring and neap tides

The spring tides are the most extreme tides of the month, with the highest rises and falls, and the neap tides are the least extreme, with the smallest. Exact timings vary around the coast, but expect them around the following dates:

Spring tides: 4th–5th and 18th–19th

Neap tides: 11th–12th and 26th–27th

In the tide timetable opposite, spring tides are shown with an asterisk.

June tide timetable for Dover

For your local high tide differences on Dover, see page 8.

	High water		*Low water*	
	Morning	Afternoon	Morning	Afternoon
1st	10.28	22.42	05.23	17.45
2nd	11.06	23.20	06.10	18.30
3rd	11.43	23.58	06.54	19.13
4th	–	12.21	07.37	19.55 *
5th	00.38	13.02	08.18	20.36 *
6th	01.20	13.47	08.59	21.19
7th	02.07	14.35	09.40	22.04
8th	02.58	15.30	10.26	22.54
9th	03.59	16.32	11.18	23.52
10th	05.10	17.39	–	12.21
11th	06.30	18.53	00.59	13.31
12th	07.46	20.06	02.07	14.40
13th	08.52	21.11	03.14	15.46
14th	09.48	22.06	04.20	16.51
15th	10.37	22.56	05.26	17.51
16th	11.22	23.42	06.23	18.42
17th	12.03	–	07.11	19.27
18th	00.24	12.42	07.51	20.07 *
19th	01.03	13.21	08.27	20.43 *
20th	01.42	14.00	09.00	21.16
21st	02.20	14.39	09.28	21.46
22nd	02.58	15.17	09.56	22.17
23rd	03.38	15.56	10.28	22.54
24th	04.22	16.39	11.07	23.38
25th	05.15	17.31	11.55	–
26th	06.15	18.32	00.35	12.57
27th	07.18	19.34	01.43	14.12
28th	08.16	20.31	02.50	15.19
29th	09.07	21.21	03.50	16.17
30th	09.53	22.08	04.46	17.12

THE SKY AT NIGHT

Moon phases

New moon – 3rd June

1st quarter – 10th June

Full moon – 17th June

3rd quarter – 25th June

In the night sky this month

16th   Close approach of the moon and Jupiter, first visible in the twilight around 21.30 at about 9 degrees above the southeastern horizon. They reach a height of 16 degrees at 00.30 in the south and set at 04.00 in the southwest.

18th   Close approach of the moon and Saturn, which rise at 23.00 over the southeastern horizon. They reach an altitude of 17 degrees in the south at 02.30 before becoming lost in the dawn at 03.00 in the southwest.

Moon rise and set

	Inverness		Padstow		
	Rise	Set	Rise	Set	
1st	04.14	19.21	04.33	19.02	
2nd	04.32	20.43	04.59	20.16	
3rd	04.57	22.03	05.31	21.29	new moon
4th	05.30	23.16	06.11	22.37	
5th	06.17	–	07.02	23.38	
6th	07.20	00.17	08.04	–	
7th	08.37	01.03	09.16	00.29	
8th	10.02	01.36	10.33	01.09	
9th	11.30	02.01	11.52	01.42	
10th	12.58	02.20	13.12	02.09	1st quarter
11th	14.24	02.36	14.30	02.33	
12th	15.50	02.51	15.47	02.56	
13th	17.15	03.06	17.03	03.18	
14th	18.38	03.22	18.19	03.42	
15th	20.00	03.41	19.32	04.09	
16th	21.16	04.05	20.42	04.41	
17th	22.24	04.37	21.45	05.18	full moon
18th	23.19	05.19	22.40	06.04	
19th	–	06.11	23.25	06.57	
20th	00.01	07.14	–	07.55	
21st	00.32	08.22	00.01	08.58	
22nd	00.56	09.34	00.31	10.03	
23rd	01.14	10.46	00.56	11.07	
24th	01.29	11.58	01.17	12.12	
25th	01.41	13.10	01.37	13.18	3rd quarter
26th	01.53	14.23	01.56	14.24	
27th	02.06	15.38	02.15	15.31	
28th	02.19	16.56	02.35	16.41	
29th	02.36	18.16	02.59	17.53	
30th	02.57	19.38	03.28	19.07	

J

NATURE

Inside the beehive in June

The beehive is reaching full strength now and it may prepare to swarm, particularly if space is running out. This is its way of reproducing itself and creating new colonies. The queen lays eggs in specially prepared queen cells, and these larvae will be fed on royal jelly – produced from the heads of the nurse bees – for 16 days. Male drone bees are also raised, their only purpose being to mate with a new queen. On a still, warm day, the old queen will leave the nest (flying for only the second time in her life) with around 60 per cent of the hive – up to 30,000 of her faithful workers all flying in a mass through the June air. The swarm will settle temporarily around a branch of a tree while scout bees search for a new home. Back in the old hive, the new queens fight for dominance, and the survivor flies from the nest with a drone bee to mate on the wing, then returns to the hive to take her place as the new queen.

Look out for...dragonflies emerging from the nymph phase

Spend some time near a pond and you may be witness to the otherworldly sight of dragonflies clinging to the base of reeds and slowly pushing their way out of their exoskeletons. Once they have fully climbed out, they will hang there for a few hours, gradually pumping up their iridescent wings and hardening their skins, before taking their first flight.

NATIVE TREES – LEAVES

OAK

ASH

BEECH

LIME

FIELD MAPLE

J

THE GARDEN

Planting by the moon

New moon to 1st quarter: 3rd–10th. Sow crops that develop below ground. Dig the soil.

1st quarter to full moon: 10th–17th. Sow crops that develop above ground. Plant seedlings and young plants.

Full moon to 3rd quarter: 17th–25th. Harvest crops for immediate eating. Harvest fruit.

3rd quarter to new moon: 25th–2nd July. Prune. Harvest for storage. Fertilise and mulch the soil.

Job of the month – plant and pinch out tomatoes

Tomato growing is a race against blight and our short season. Use sturdy supports with newly planted-out tomatoes, which grow much bigger than you expect. Start feeding them every week and watering daily. Religiously pinch out the side shoots that arise from between the leaf joints, forcing the plant to develop one main stem only, which allows ripening energy to be concentrated on a few trusses of tomatoes.

Glut of the month – strawberries

Once you spot that your strawberries are ripe, leave them for a day before picking, and then maybe for another. The extra little time will set them leagues above tasteless supermarket fruits. Less ripe fruits are vastly improved by tumbling with lemon juice and a little icing sugar and leaving for a few hours.

- **Eton mess:** Whip cream, crush meringues, and tumble with perfectly ripe strawberries for classic Eton mess.
- **Strawberry and watermelon slushie:** Cube and freeze a watermelon overnight, then blend with several handfuls of strawberries and the juice of a lemon.
- **Roasted strawberries:** Mix them with a splash of apple juice and a little honey, and bake at 190°C, Gas Mark 5 for 15 minutes or until the juices run. Eat them hot spooned over ice cream or cool on Greek yoghurt.

Flower of the month – rose

Latin name: *Rosa* (Latin, meaning 'rose').
Common name: rose.

June is the month of roses. This is high summer, and from every other front garden come wafts of musky, spicy, fruity or just good old-fashioned floral. You can't walk down the street without stopping to cup the soft, cool petals to your nose. Some roses putter on throughout summer, some have a phase one and a phase two, some have just one spectacular display, but all will be flowering their hearts out in June.

Where to start with the symbolism of the rose? It can represent romantic love, patriotism, political struggle. Everyone claims it, and it means something different each time. Christians see it as a flower of harmony, and of the Virgin Mary. In Texas, a yellow rose means undying love. In tarot, the rose is a symbol of balance. To the British Labour Party, a red rose has long associations with European socialism and harks back to the sentiment of the textile workers' strike-song 'Bread and Roses': 'Hearts starve as well as bodies, give us bread but give us roses.'

This is not the time for planting, but it is the time for looking, sniffing and choosing. Make notes now and buy and plant in autumn. Roses are easy to grow but they particularly like deep, rich and clay soils and are less happy on thin and sandy ones. They are greedy, but will flower for a great many years if treated well.

A SONG FOR A ROSE

'Rose in June'
Traditional

This pretty song was collected by Bob Copper, a member
of the Copper Family – folk singers who passed songs down
through the generations. Bob also acted as a collector and
recorded this from George Fosbury in Hampshire in 1954.
It is a song of love, petals and of wandering and picking
in midsummer.

Was down in the val-ley, the val-ley so deep to
pick some fine ros-es to keep my love sweet so let it be ear-ly
late or noon I'll en-joy my rose in June.

The violets make the meadows smell sweet,
But none with my roses can compete.

   Chorus:
   So let it be early, late or noon,
   I will enjoy my rose in June.

The rose in June's not half so sweet
As kisses where true lovers meet.

   Chorus

Then I will drive my flock to the fold,
Let the weather blow warm or cold.

   Chorus

Then I'll cut down the sweet myrtle tree,
To make a fine bower for Sally and me.

   Chorus

Of every sweet flower that grows,
None can compare to my blooming rose.

   Chorus

THE KITCHEN

Cheese of the month – Flower Marie

Flower Marie is an unpasteurised sheep's milk cheese from West Sussex modelled on the Fleur du Maquis sheep's cheese of Corsica. The Golden Cross Company makes it all year round using milk from a local herd and from a second herd in Warwickshire. The batch that is ready at midsummer has been made from rich grassy milk at lambing time, when the milk is especially plentiful. It is mixed with a vegetarian rennet and the resulting curds are hand-layered into small square moulds, and left to drain. This creates a good structure and makes for a dense cheese that doesn't collapse when cooked. Penicillium mould helps each cheese to develop a white, bloomy rind similar to that of a Camembert or a Brie. Flower Marie is matured for about two weeks before wrapping, but will keep developing for five weeks, becoming more gooey in the centre. It has a soft and rich texture and sweet, subtle and slightly citrusy flavour when young, developing a stronger flavour as it ages.

In season

Strawberries, raspberries, cherries, apricots and gooseberries are at their best this month. Blackcurrants, white currants and red currants are fruiting.

Broad beans, globe artichokes, French beans, peas, lettuce, Florence fennel and carrots are all starting to be picked, and you may dig some new potatoes on your own vegetable patch. Watercress, spring onions and radishes are all ready.

Summer herbs – basil, mint, chives and dill – are fresh and perfect now.

Crab, mackerel and sardines are plentiful.

Fresh, unmatured cheeses such as ewes' curd, chèvre, ricotta and feta are at their finest now, as herds are eating abundant young grass and herbs.

RECIPES

Jam making

Jam making time is here. Fill the air with the glorious scent of juicy fruit and sugar, and bottle yourself a bit of summer.

Different fruits have different amounts of pectin, the substance that holds jam together. With low-pectin fruits you have a choice: buy jam sugar, which contains pectin; add pectin separately; mix low-pectin fruits with high-pectin fruits; or add lemon juice. The latter can often be enough to draw out the natural pectin in the fruit and create a good set. This generally makes for a nicer texture than using commercial pectin, which can create a jelly-like consistency. Note that underripe fruit generally contains more pectin than fully ripe fruit.

High-pectin fruits: Apples, crab apples, quince, plums, gooseberries, currants, blackberries (underripe), citrus fruit.

Low-pectin fruits: Strawberries, apricots, peaches, raspberries, cherries, blueberries.

Equipment

Large preserving pan

Sugar thermometer

A few saucers, chilled in the refrigerator

Ladle

Sterilised jam funnel

Sterilised jars with lids

Waxed paper circles

Labels

Makes about six 300ml jars

Ingredients

1kg fruit (perhaps mixed high- and low-pectin)

1kg sugar

Juice of 1 lemon/pectin (up to 13g per 1kg sugar)

Method

Wash, peel and stone your fruit, and remove green parts. Put the fruit in the preserving pan and place over a very low heat. The fruit will immediately start to release its juices (you can add a splash of water to get it going if it seems dry). Bring to a very gentle simmer and cook until the fruit is tender, up to 1 hour. Add the sugar and the lemon juice, or pectin if using, and continue to heat gently, stirring, until all of the sugar has dissolved. Turn the heat up to bring the fruit to a rolling boil, then stop stirring completely. At first the bubbles will be quite wild and random but gradually it will settle into more of a gentle blip, and the bubbles will start to take on a glassier look. Take the temperature with a sugar thermometer, and test the jam when it reaches 104°C.

To test if it has reached setting point, remove the pan from the heat, take one of the saucers out of the refrigerator, put a small blob of jam on it and return it to the fridge for a minute. Run your finger through the centre: if the jam wrinkles ahead of your finger and if you leave a clear channel through the jam then it is at setting point; if not, then return the pan to the heat and keep boiling and testing every minute or two. When you have achieved a set, leave the jam to cool for 10 minutes and then use a ladle and jam funnel to fill the jars. Place a waxed paper disc on the top of each jar of jam, and seal. Label when it has cooled.

Buttermilk scones with orange blossom and honey butter

Buttermilk is used in scones because it is acidic and reacts with baking powder to create a good rise and make really soft, fluffy scones. If you don't have buttermilk, fake it by adding a tablespoon of lemon juice to whole milk 10 minutes before using. The milk will start to curdle, and then it is ready to be used. If making both the butter and the scones, prepare the butter first: ideally you want warm scones to meet cold butter.

Makes about 10 scones

Ingredients

For the orange blossom and honey butter

120g salted butter, softened

Zest of 1 orange

2 teaspoons orange flower water

2 tablespoons runny honey

For the scones

225g self-raising flour, plus extra for dusting

½ teaspoon salt

1 teaspoon baking powder

50g butter

150ml buttermilk (or whole milk and lemon juice – see opposite)

Milk, to glaze

Method

To make the honey butter, use a wooden spoon to cream the butter until soft, then add the zest, flower water and honey. Cream until everything is thoroughly mixed and the butter is light and creamy. Spoon it into a small bowl and refrigerate.

To make the scones, preheat your oven to 230°C, Gas Mark 8. In a large bowl, mix the flour, salt and baking powder, then rub in the butter until the mixture resembles breadcrumbs. Pour in the buttermilk. Stir, bringing everything together into a dough. Turn out onto a floured surface and knead briefly, then roll out to about 2.5cm thick. Use a 7cm cutter to stamp out rounds, and place them on a baking sheet lined with baking parchment. Brush the tops with milk and bake for 8–10 minutes or until browned on top. Serve warm.

July

The naming of July

> Iuchar (Scots Gaelic)
> Julie (Scots/Ulster Scots)
> Iúil (Irish Gaelic)
> Jerry-souree (Manx)
> Gorffennaf (Welsh)
> Gortheren (Cornish)
> Juilet (Jèrriais)

Julius Caesar named July 'Julius' after himself in 46 BC, as a pat on the back for reforming the Roman calendar and creating the (you guessed it) Julian calendar. Before this, July was known as Quintilis, the fifth month (the first month then being March), but no trace of Quintilis has remained in the names of the month, while several are based on Julius. The Manx Jerry-souree may look as if it is related but, in fact, *jerry* means 'end' and *souree* means 'summer'. This seems impossibly pessimistic to our modern way of thinking but is related to a more complex understanding of the agricultural patterns of the year than to any more romantic sense of summer (or indeed to the temperature). Summer was considered the months of growth – May, June and July – and August was when crops switched their energies to fruiting and ripening, and the time for the first harvests. Hence July was seen as the last month of summer. Similarly, the Welsh Gorffennaf is from *gorfen* meaning 'end' and *haf* meaning 'summer'. The Scots Gaelic Iuchar and the Irish Gaelic Iúil have another root entirely – they are thought to be related to *fiuch*, meaning 'to boil or seethe', presumably relating to those sweltering Outer Hebrides summers.

A CORNISH FOLK TALE FOR JULY

The curse of the Doom Bar

There was once a time, many years ago, when Padstow was a deep and wide natural harbour, blessed with the protection of a beautiful mermaid, or merry maid, as they are called in Cornwall. Large boats sailed in and out freely, and the harbour and town were prosperous and busy. But as any sailor knows, mermaids are not to be trifled with, and these blissful years were not to last. One day the mermaid was sitting on the rocks at Hawker's Cove combing her long golden hair, when she noticed a young man walking among the rocks, holding a gun. He was a local man, a sailor called Tristram Bird, and was out hunting seals. The mermaid was unhappy to see this and decided to distract him in order to save her seal friends, and so to catch his attention she started singing the most beautiful song. Tristram forgot his hunting and fell instantly in love with her, and he ran to her begging for her hand in marriage. But she laughed and rejected him, telling him that she only wished to stop him from shooting the seals. At this he flew into a rage and shot her instead! With her dying breath she cursed the harbour with a 'bar of doom', and picked up a handful of sand, flinging it from Hawker's Cove to Trebetherick Bay. That night a storm blew up and by morning a sand bar lay across the bay, strewn with wrecked boats and the bodies of sailors.

The second Sunday in July – this year, it falls on the 14th July – is Sea Sunday. This is the day the Catholic Church offers services and blessings for seafarers and their families, and raises funds for the Apostleship of the Sea, often known as Stella Maris, which offers ministry and support for sailors in ports. Stella Maris, or Star of the Sea, is another name for the Virgin Mary, who is believed to be the guide and protector of seafarers – though possibly not those who go about shooting mermaids.

WEATHER

Summer hailstorms

Hail in summer always feels like a symptom of our crazy, out-of-sync weather but, in fact, hail is naturally a summer phenomenon. The most intense hailstorms occur between May and September, with a defined peak in July. Hail forms in giant thunderclouds, cumulonimbus, which grow to great, towering heights in the summer as they are fed by the hot ground creating thermals that lift water vapour high into the air. The tops of these massive clouds are freezing cold, and here drops of water turn to ice crystals. As they start to fall through the cloud, they make contact with other water droplets, which cling to the surface, and the strong updraughts within a cumulonimbus cloud then whisk them back up to the top and freeze them again. This circulation can happen numerous times, until the hail pellets grow too heavy, and fall to earth.

Average temperatures (°C):	Inverness 14, Padstow 15
Average sunshine hours per day:	Inverness 5, Padstow 7
Average days of rainfall:	Inverness 18, Padstow 20
Average rainfall total (mm):	Inverness 20, Padstow 61

Day length

During the course of July, day length decreases by:

1 hour 30 minutes (to 16 hours 24 minutes) – Inverness
1 hour 3 minutes (to 15 hours 20 minutes) – Padstow

Aphelion is on 4th July at 23.10. This is the moment in the year when the earth is farthest from the sun.

Sunrise and set

	Inverness		*Padstow*	
	Rise	Set	Rise	Set
1st	04.23	22.17	05.11	21.35
2nd	04.24	22.17	05.12	21.34
3rd	04.25	22.16	05.13	21.34
4th	04.26	22.15	05.13	21.33
5th	04.27	22.14	05.14	21.33
6th	04.28	22.14	05.15	21.32
7th	04.29	22.13	05.16	21.32
8th	04.30	22.12	05.17	21.31
9th	04.32	22.11	05.18	21.31
10th	04.33	22.10	05.19	21.30
11th	04.34	22.08	05.20	21.29
12th	04.36	22.07	05.21	21.28
13th	04.37	22.06	05.22	21.28
14th	04.39	22.05	05.23	21.27
15th	04.40	22.03	05.24	21.26
16th	04.42	22.02	05.25	21.25
17th	04.44	22.00	05.26	21.24
18th	04.45	21.59	05.27	21.23
19th	04.47	21.57	05.29	21.22
20th	04.49	21.55	05.30	21.21
21st	04.51	21.54	05.31	21.19
22nd	04.53	21.52	05.32	21.18
23rd	04.54	21.50	05.34	21.17
24th	04.56	21.48	05.35	21.16
25th	04.58	21.46	05.36	21.14
26th	05.00	21.45	05.38	21.13
27th	05.02	21.43	05.39	21.12
28th	05.04	21.41	05.40	21.10
29th	05.06	21.39	05.42	21.09
30th	05.08	21.36	05.43	21.07
31st	05.10	21.34	05.45	21.06

J

THE SEA

Average sea temperature

Isle of Lewis:	12.7°C
Whitby:	15.1°C
Belfast:	13.6°C
Cork:	15.7°C
Swansea:	15.8°C
Brighton:	15.4°C
Falmouth:	16.4°C

Spring and neap tides

The spring tides are the most extreme tides of the month, with the highest rises and falls, and the neap tides are the least extreme, with the smallest. Exact timings vary around the coast, but expect them around the following dates:

Spring tides: 4th–5th and 17th–18th

Neap tides: 10th–11th and 26th–27th

In the tide timetable opposite, spring tides are shown with an asterisk.

July tide timetable for Dover

For your local high tide differences on Dover, see page 8.

	High water		Low water	
	Morning	Afternoon	Morning	Afternoon
1st	10.38	22.54	05.39	18.03
2nd	11.22	23.40	06.30	18.52
3rd	–	12.07	07.19	19.40
4th	00.26	12.53	08.08	20.29 *
5th	01.13	13.40	08.56	21.17 *
6th	02.02	14.29	09.42	22.06
7th	02.53	15.21	10.28	22.54
8th	03.48	16.15	11.14	23.44
9th	04.48	17.12	–	12.05
10th	05.53	18.15	00.38	13.01
11th	07.05	19.26	01.37	14.04
12th	08.17	20.39	02.40	15.10
13th	09.21	21.45	03.46	16.18
14th	10.17	22.42	04.55	17.24
15th	11.05	23.30	05.58	18.21
16th	11.48	–	06.49	19.08
17th	00.12	12.27	07.31	19.49 *
18th	00.49	13.04	08.07	20.25 *
19th	01.25	13.41	08.38	20.56
20th	02.00	14.16	09.06	21.26
21st	02.33	14.48	09.33	21.55
22nd	03.03	15.15	10.04	22.28
23rd	03.32	15.46	10.38	23.04
24th	04.06	16.26	11.17	23.46
25th	04.52	17.18	–	12.02
26th	06.01	18.28	00.39	13.02
27th	07.25	19.44	01.51	14.25
28th	08.32	20.50	03.08	15.39
29th	09.29	21.47	04.14	16.42
30th	10.20	22.40	05.14	17.40
31st	11.09	23.29	06.10	18.35

A SAILOR'S SONG

'The Mermaid'
Traditional

'The Mermaid' is one of the 'Child Ballads' (number 289) collected by folklorist Francis James Child in England and Scotland in the second half of the 19th century. It is a sea ballad – sung by sailors during resting times – rather than a sea shanty, or working song. As is often the case in folklore, the sighting of the mermaid is a sign of impending disaster.

'Twas a Fri-da-y morn when we set sail, Our
ship not far from the land, When we did es spy a
fair mer-maid, With a comb and a glass in her
hand, her hand, her hand. With a comb and a glass in her hand. Oh the
o-cean waves do roll, And the stor-my winds do blow, And as
we jol-ly sai-lor boys were up, were up a-loft, And the
land lub-bers ly-ing down be-low, be-low, be-low And the
land lub-bers ly-ing down be-low.

Up spoke the captain of our gallant ship
And a brave old skipper was he
'This fishy mermaid has warned me of our doom
We shall sink to the bottom of the sea, the sea, the sea
We shall sink to the bottom of the sea.'

> *Chorus:*
> *Oh the ocean waves do roll*
> *And the stormy winds do blow*
> *And as we jolly sailor boys were up, were up aloft*
> *And the landlubbers lying down below, below, below*
> *And the landlubbers lying down below.*

Up spoke the first mate of our gallant ship
And a well-spoken man was he
'I have me a wife in Salem by the sea
And tonight she a widow will be, will be, will be
And tonight she a widow will be.'

> *Chorus*

Then up spoke the cabinboy, of our gallant ship
And a fair-haired lad was he
'I'm not quite sure I can spell mermaid
But I'm going to the bottom of the sea, the sea, the sea
But I'm going to the bottom of the sea.'

> *Chorus*

Then three times around spun our gallant ship
And three times around spun she
Three times around spun our gallant ship
And she sank to the bottom of the sea, the sea, the sea
And she sank to the bottom of the sea.

> *Chorus*

SEASHELLS

VARIEGATED
SCALLOP

COMMON
ORMER

PAINTED
TOP SHELL

STRIPED
VENUS CLAM

COMMON
WHELK

THE SKY AT NIGHT

Moon phases

New moon – 2nd July

1st quarter – 9th July

Full moon – 16th July

3rd quarter – 25th July

In the night sky this month

13th	Close approach of the moon and Jupiter, first visible in the twilight at around 22.00 at about 15 degrees above the southeastern horizon. They reach a height of 16 degrees at 22.30 in the south and set at 02.00 in the southwest.
15th	Close approach of the moon and Saturn, which appear as dusk falls at about 22.00 in the southeast at an altitude of 9 degrees. Maximum altitude of 16 degrees occurs at 00.30 in the south, and they set at around 04.00 in the southwest.
16th	Partial lunar eclipse. However, it may be difficult to see. The moon rises partially eclipsed at 21.00 in the southeast. It reaches its most eclipsed (65 per cent) at 22.30 but at only 9 degrees above the horizon. The eclipse ends at midnight with the moon at 14 degrees in the south.

J

Moon rise and set

	Inverness		Padstow		
	Rise	Set	Rise	Set	
1st	03.26	20.56	04.04	20.19	
2nd	04.06	22.04	04.50	21.25	new moon
3rd	05.03	22.58	05.48	22.21	
4th	06.16	23.37	06.58	23.07	
5th	07.41	–	08.16	23.44	
6th	09.11	00.06	09.37	–	
7th	10.42	00.27	10.58	00.14	
8th	12.10	00.45	12.18	00.39	
9th	13.37	01.00	13.36	01.02	1st quarter
10th	15.01	01.15	14.53	01.24	
11th	16.25	01.30	16.08	01.47	
12th	17.46	01.48	17.21	02.13	
13th	19.03	02.09	18.31	02.42	
14th	20.13	02.38	19.36	03.17	
15th	21.12	03.15	20.33	03.59	
16th	21.59	04.03	21.21	04.49	full moon
17th	22.34	05.02	22.01	05.45	
18th	23.00	06.08	22.33	06.46	
19th	23.20	07.19	22.59	07.50	
20th	23.36	08.31	23.22	08.55	
21st	23.49	09.43	23.42	10.00	
22nd	–	10.55	–	11.05	
23rd	00.01	12.07	00.01	12.10	
24th	00.13	13.20	00.19	13.16	
25th	00.26	14.35	00.39	14.23	3rd quarter
26th	00.40	15.52	01.00	15.33	
27th	00.58	17.12	01.26	16.44	
28th	01.22	18.30	01.57	17.56	
29th	01.56	19.43	02.37	19.05	
30th	02.44	20.45	03.29	20.06	
31st	03.50	21.32	04.34	20.58	

Meteor shower of the month – the Delta Aquariids

July's meteor show comes courtesy of a comet from a group
known as the sungrazers, whose orbits take them within a few
thousand kilometres of the sun before flinging them back out
into deep space. These comets are often in groups, possibly
because the original parent body has been ripped apart by the
massive forces they encounter, but it is Comet 96P/Machholz
whose dust trails spark through the July night as the Delta
Aquariids. The shower this year peaks on the night and pre-
dawn of 28th–29th July, when a waning crescent moon should
allow for good viewing, but it also rumbles on from around
12th July to 23rd August each year and may even coincide
with the Perseids in August. If you find yourself witnessing
a particularly impressive meteor show and want to know
the difference between the two, Delta Aquariid meteors
will radiate from the constellation Aquarius, while Perseid
meteors radiate from Perseus.

J

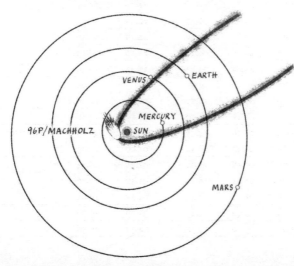

NATURE

Inside the beehive in July

The colony is now at full strength, with thousands of bees setting out all day every day to reap the bountiful summer flowers. Wild blackberry, clover, rosebay willowherb, poppy, thistle, red campion, meadow cranesbill and gardens full of flowers are all providing nectar for the summer's honey. At the end of June and the beginning of July, lime trees start to flower, providing a major source of nectar, particularly for city bees. This pollen makes a dark amber, complex, slightly minty honey. Some farmers grow borage on a large scale for its seed, and honey here will be very pale and clear. Whatever its look and flavour, the race is on to fill the hive with honey to see it through winter. Each individual bee will produce approximately $^1/_{12}$th of a teaspoon of honey in its lifetime, which lasts for about 6 weeks, and an average colony will need 25kg of surplus honey to survive to the following spring.

Look out for...moths

This is a good time to go moth spotting. At dusk on a warm, dry, calm evening, hang an old white bed sheet over the washing line, shine a lamp onto it from behind, then wait for poplar hawk-moths, cinnabar moths, silver-ground carpets, swallow-tailed moths and others to visit.

THE GARDEN

Planting by the moon

New moon to 1st quarter: 2nd–9th. Sow crops that develop below ground. Dig the soil.

1st quarter to full moon: 9th–16th. Sow crops that develop above ground. Plant seedlings and young plants.

Full moon to 3rd quarter: 16th–25th. Harvest crops for immediate eating. Harvest fruit.

3rd quarter to new moon: 25th–1st August. Prune. Harvest for storage. Fertilise and mulch the soil.

Job of the month – look after your pond

Sunlight and warmth can lead to summer problems for ponds: water level dropping, low oxygen levels, and algal growth. Pull out pond weed using a rake, top up (ideally with rainwater) and consider a small fountain to keep oxygen levels up.

Glut of the month – runner beans

Runner beans are one of the great gluts of the vegetable-gardening year. Pick them young and often to prevent them from quickly growing into stringy monsters.

- **Crudités with bagna cauda:** Cut 250g butter into cubes. Melt a quarter of it in a pan. Add 5 cloves crushed garlic and 12 anchovies, and cook slowly until mushy. Start whisking the mixture and add the cubes of butter, one at a time, whisking and melting them in. When all is melted, trickle in 250ml extra virgin olive oil, whisking as you go. Serve warm with crunchy raw runner beans to dip.
- **Fasolakia:** This is a Greek side dish of slow-cooked green beans. Fry onions gently in olive oil then add cubes of potatoes, tomatoes and sliced runner beans. Cover and cook over low heat for 40 minutes.
- **Runner beans with garlic and lemon:** Quick-fry thinly sliced runner beans with garlic, then squeeze over the juice of a lemon and sprinkle with salt.

Flower of the month – oxeye daisy

Latin name: *Leucanthemum vulgare* (*Leucanthemum* from the Greek *leukos*, meaning 'white', and *anthemon*, meaning 'flower'; *vulgare* meaning 'common').
Common names: moon penny, moon daisy, dog daisy.

Happy, sunny oxeye daisies once filled the countryside in July, the last hurrah of the hay meadows before they turned their attention to seed. The old common names of moon penny and moon daisy arose because of the flower's ability to glow in moonlight, and what a sight a daisy-rich meadow must have been on a moonlit July evening. Now they are most likely to be spotted in hedgerows, which so often act as the final vestiges of the habitats that once surrounded them. Modern agriculture has all but done for the meadows, but oxeye daisies and their companions – valerian, hedge bedstraw, common toadflax and all – cling on at the margins. You may even see diminutive oxeye daisies on cliff edges, in dwarf forms because of the salt-laden wind.

If you wanted to start a meadow of your own, even a small-scale one, the dependable and spectacular oxeye daisy is the place to start – sow the seed in autumn. Alternatively, plant it in a border, where this beautiful wildling will hold its own among the cultivated perennials.

THE KITCHEN

Cheese of the month – Beenleigh Blue

Beenleigh Blue was originally conceived as the British answer
to Roquefort, but even though it has Roquefort's blue veining
it has developed into quite a different cheese, which is more
delicately sweet and minerally than Roquefort. Made by
Ticklemore Cheese, based in Devon, using ewes' milk from a
farm in Somerset, Beenleigh Blue is only made in the spring
and early summer. This is when the ewes are just out, grazing
on grass and clover leys, and the milk is just right. As the
summer wears on, the milk becomes more fatty, and this fat
inhibits the growth of the blue mould. The cheese changes
distinctly throughout its short season. The earliest of the year's
cheeses, which were ready in May, were light, citrussy, flinty
and mineral, while the later cheeses are richer and creamier
with a more robust, earthy and intense flavour. This is the last
month of the year that Beenleigh Blue is made, and the cheeses
produced now will be ready into autumn.

In season

There is no shortage of garden veg this month. **New potatoes,
young carrots, salads, peas, asparagus, globe artichokes,
mangetouts, spring onions, lettuce, runner beans, French beans,
celery** and **rocket** are all ready, with **courgettes** in full-blown
glut. There may be a few **broad beans** around but this is the end
of their season.

Fruit too is varied and at its peak. **Apricots, peaches**
and **nectarines, cherries, raspberries, currants, gooseberries,
blueberries** and **strawberries** are all in season. The first **plums**
and **blackberries** are ripening.

Mint, basil and **dill** are the herbs of the moment. Edible
flowers are appearing on the vegetable patch, including
calendula flowers, courgette flowers and **nasturtium flowers.**

Sea bass, mackerel, sardine and **crab** are all plentiful.

The short season for **samphire** has begun.

All of the fresh, young cheeses are wonderful at the moment
as milk is produced from animals on plentiful, fresh grass.

J

RECIPES

Summer vegetable and feta pie

This is very clearly based on spanakopita, but with half the veg patch thrown in – got to make the most of those gluts. It makes good, if crumbly, picnic fare: do not eat in the car.

Serves 6
Ingredients
500g spinach
1 onion
50ml extra virgin olive oil
100g French beans, trimmed
100g broad beans, steamed and double podded
100g fresh peas
Leaves from a few sprigs of mint, finely chopped
400g feta cheese, crumbled
Skin of half a preserved lemon, finely chopped
3 large eggs, beaten
10 sheets filo pastry
50g melted butter
1 tablespoon sesame seeds
1 teaspoon sea salt flakes

Method
Wash the spinach well and place as much of it as you can into a saucepan with a lid, then cover and place over a medium heat. The spinach will steam in the water that is clinging to its leaves and collapse fairly quickly. Once it has, tip it out into a colander and repeat with any leaves that didn't fit in the first batch. Let the two spinach batches cool in the colander, then squeeze out the excess water. Transfer to a chopping board and chop roughly, then put it back in the colander for a final squeeze. Set aside.

Chop the onion and soften it in the olive oil over low to medium heat for at least 10 minutes, until translucent. Tip it into a large bowl then add the spinach, vegetables (the uncooked ones will cook enough in the oven), mint, feta cheese, preserved lemon and eggs. Mix well.

Preheat the oven to 200°C, Gas Mark 6 and place a baking sheet on the middle shelf. Unroll the filo pastry and place it on a flat surface, covered in a slightly damp tea towel to prevent it from drying out. Loosely push a piece of baking parchment into a 20cm loose-bottomed tart tin or cake tin. Lay the first sheet of filo in the tin, pushing it down into the corners. Paint it all over with the melted butter and then lay in the next sheet, at a slight angle, and paint that with the butter. Continue until all ten sheets are in the tin, overlapping each other.

Pile the filling into the centre and smooth it out, then fold in the last sheet of filo you laid in the tin. Paint it with butter, then repeat for the previous one, and so on, until all of the butter-covered sheets of filo are folded over the top. Paint the top with the last of the butter and sprinkle over the sesame seeds and sea salt. Bake for about 40 minutes, or until the filo pastry is crisp and golden brown. Serve just warm or at room temperature.

J

Homemade lemonade

The most refreshing summer drink, sharp and sweet. Start this the day before you are going to drink it (or sell it on the street – recommended retail price 50p a cup).

Makes about 1.5 litres
Ingredients
8 lemons
1.4 litres boiling water
150g caster sugar
Chilled fizzy water, to taste (optional)
Ice (optional)
Measure of vodka (optional)

Method

Thinly pare the zest of half the lemons, taking care to take as little of the pith as possible. Place all of the pieces of zest into a large bowl and pour over the freshly boiled water. After a few minutes add the sugar and stir in, then squeeze in the juice of the lemons. Stir well then leave to sit overnight. The next day, strain through a colander, pour into bottles and chill. Serve neat or diluted with fizzy water and lots of ice, or add a measure of vodka to turn it into a refreshing sundowner.

Grilled sea bass baps with buttered samphire

Samphire is sometimes known as 'sea asparagus' but really it is entirely its own vegetable, succulent and salty. Its season is brief in the extreme. For July and August only, you may find it at a fishmonger's, or can forage it yourself from mudflats and estuary edges if you have the local know-how. It is brilliant with every fish and is great raw or lightly cooked, so get in to the easy habit of making use of it while it is around. If you find yourself throwing a beach barbecue this month or next, make up a jar of the sauce beforehand, grill whole fish over the coals (mackerel would also be good), and wedge chunks of fish into the baps with handfuls of raw samphire and a dollop of crème fraîche. Otherwise, here is the recipe for the (only marginally fancier) indoor version.

Serves 4

Ingredients

200ml full-fat crème fraîche

Small handful of parsley, finely chopped

Juice of half a lemon

4 sea bass fillets (or 2 whole sea bass, gutted and cleaned, if you are barbecuing)

A little olive oil

40g butter

100g samphire

4 soft white baps

Salt and pepper

Method

Mix the crème fraîche, parsley and lemon juice. Score the skin of the sea bass fillets several times with a sharp knife, then pour a little olive oil into a frying pan and heat to a moderately high heat. Season the fillets with salt on each side and then put them into the pan, skin side down. Press them with a fish slice to stop them from curling. After a few minutes the skin should be crispy; turn the fillets over and cook for 1 minute, then remove from the heat, cover with a lid or plate, and set aside. Heat the butter in a small saucepan and add the samphire. Cook it for a few minutes just to heat it through, then remove from the heat. Split the baps, fill with the sea bass, samphire and crème fraîche, and serve hot.

August

- **1**   Lammas/Lughnasadh (pagan)
- **2**   2nd–26th: Edinburgh Festival
- **5**   August bank holiday, Scotland, Republic of Ireland
- **9**   9th–14th: Hajj (Muslim)
- **10**   10th–11th: Tisha B'Av (Jewish)
- **11**   11th–15th: Eid al-Adha (Muslim)
- **12**   The Glorious Twelfth – grouse-shooting season begins
- **15**   The Assumption of Mary (Christian)
- **24**   24th–26th: Notting Hill Carnival, London
- **24**   Krishna Janmashtami – Krishna's birthday (Hindu)
- **26**   Summer bank holiday, England, Wales, Northern Ireland
- **31**   Al-Hijra – Islamic New Year (Muslim)

The naming of August

> Lùnastal (Scots Gaelic)
> August (Scots/Ulster Scots)
> Lúnasa (Irish Gaelic)
> Luanistyn (Manx)
> Awst (Welsh)
> Est (Cornish)
> Août (Jèrriais)

After Julius Caesar started the Julian calendar reform and rewarded himself with a month (July), along came Augustus Caesar to complete the job, and so he gave himself a month, too, hence August. Most of the languages of the British Isles have variants on this as their names for August (including the very French Août in Jèrriais). However, Scots Gaelic, Irish Gaelic and Manx all name the month after the Gaelic festival of Lughnasadh, one of the four Gaelic agricultural markers of the year (along with Imbolc, Beltane and Samhain). Lughnasadh is the first harvest festival of the year and particularly celebrates the first cuts of wheat and the first fruits: nature has shifted from growth to ripening.

AN IRISH MYTH FOR AUGUST

Lugh and the harvest

Lugh was a god of ancient Ireland, and a member of the Tuatha Dé Danann, the race of bold and brave gods that ruled over pre-Christian Ireland. His festival, Lughnasadh, falls on 1st August – roughly halfway between the summer solstice and the autumn equinox. Until well into the 20th century it was widely observed throughout Ireland, Scotland and the Isle of Man as one of the seasonal Gaelic festivals, and may have been even more widespread. It has equivalents in the Welsh festival of Gwyl Awst and the English Lammas.

Tall, beautiful and multi-skilled, Lugh was closely associated with the month of August and with agriculture and the harvest. He has been adopted by modern Pagans as a sun god, but the old myths show a stronger connection to grain and to farming. He defeated the cruel god Bres in battle and in return for sparing his life forced Bres to teach the Tuatha Dé Danann the skills of agriculture. Lugh outwitted the fearsome Crom Cruach, who was determined to keep all of the harvest for himself, and Lugh seized it for mankind before doing battle with another evil figure representing blight. He created Lughnasadh as a tribute to his foster mother, the goddess Tailtiu, who died of exhaustion after clearing the forests and plains of Ireland to allow agriculture to flourish. These legends clearly arose from the dawning of agriculture in ancient Ireland.

Lughnasadh has traditionally marked the beginning of the harvest season. The ceremonial cutting of the first sheaf of corn, an offering of the first fruits – bilberries and blackberries – feasting and athletic contests, and the climbing of hills are all part of its traditions. The Puck Fair in County Kerry and the Reek Sunday pilgrimage to the top of Croagh Patrick may be remnants of Lughnasadh traditions, and many Neo-Pagans will mark the day with a gathering and with bread, ale and berries to celebrate the first harvest.

A

WEATHER

Offshore winds, onshore winds and surf

If we only get into the sea once a year, August is the month. It is holiday time and in most parts of the country the sea is as warm as it is going to get. If you are just an occasional bodyboarder or surfer it makes sense to go out during nice, fun, easy waves, and the direction of the wind will have some impact on this. An onshore wind is one that is blowing from the sea in towards the land, and it can make surfing conditions tricky. It makes for messier, choppier waves and encourages waves to break sooner, which can mean that those who want to stay close to the shore miss them completely. An offshore wind – from the land out to sea – cleans up waves and slows wave breaking down, bringing the break closer to the shore and so making waves easier to catch.

Average temperatures (°C):	Inverness 14, Padstow 16
Average sunshine hours per day:	Inverness 5, Padstow 6
Average days of rainfall:	Inverness 20, Padstow 21
Average rainfall total (mm):	Inverness 30, Padstow 86

Day length

During the course of August, day length decreases by:

2 hours 18 minutes (to 16 hours 24 minutes) – Inverness
1 hour 47 minutes (to 13 hours 35 minutes) – Padstow

Sunrise and set

	Inverness		Padstow	
	Rise	Set	Rise	Set
1st	05.12	21.32	05.46	21.04
2nd	05.14	21.30	05.48	21.03
3rd	05.16	21.28	05.49	21.01
4th	05.18	21.26	05.50	20.59
5th	05.20	21.23	05.52	20.58
6th	05.22	21.21	05.53	20.56
7th	05.24	21.19	05.55	20.54
8th	05.26	21.16	05.56	20.52
9th	05.28	21.14	05.58	20.51
10th	05.30	21.12	05.59	20.49
11th	05.33	21.09	06.01	20.47
12th	05.35	21.07	06.02	20.45
13th	05.37	21.04	06.04	20.43
14th	05.39	21.02	06.05	20.42
15th	05.41	20.59	06.07	20.40
16th	05.43	20.57	06.08	20.38
17th	05.45	20.54	06.10	20.36
18th	05.47	20.52	06.11	20.34
19th	05.49	20.49	06.13	20.32
20th	05.51	20.47	06.15	20.30
21st	05.54	20.44	06.16	20.28
22nd	05.56	20.42	06.18	20.26
23rd	05.58	20.39	06.19	20.24
24th	06.00	20.36	06.21	20.22
25th	06.02	20.34	06.22	20.20
26th	06.04	20.31	06.24	20.18
27th	06.06	20.28	06.25	20.15
28th	06.08	20.26	06.27	20.13
29th	06.10	20.23	06.28	20.11
30th	06.13	20.20	06.30	20.09
31st	06.15	20.18	06.31	20.07

A

THE SEA

Average sea temperature

Isle of Lewis:	13.3°C
Whitby:	15.7°C
Belfast:	14.2°C
Cork:	16.4°C
Swansea:	16.7°C
Brighton:	16.9°C
Falmouth:	17.1°C

Spring and neap tides

The spring tides are the most extreme tides of the month, with the highest rises and falls, and the neap tides are the least extreme, with the smallest. Exact timings vary around the coast, but expect them around the following dates:

Spring tides: 2nd–3rd and 16th–17th

Neap tides: 8th–9th and 24th–25th

In the tide timetable opposite, spring tides are shown with an asterisk.

August tide timetable for Dover

For your local high tide differences on Dover, see page 8.

| | High water | | Low water | |
	Morning	Afternoon	Morning	Afternoon
1st	11.57	–	07.06	19.30
2nd	00.17	12.43	08.01	20.23 *
3rd	01.04	13.29	08.51	21.13 *
4th	01.51	14.15	09.36	21.59
5th	02.39	15.03	10.17	22.41
6th	03.28	15.52	10.57	23.24
7th	04.20	16.44	11.39	00.09
8th	05.16	17.41	–	12.27
9th	06.21	18.47	01.02	13.27
10th	07.37	20.07	02.06	14.36
11th	08.55	21.31	03.15	15.50
12th	10.01	22.35	04.29	17.05
13th	10.52	23.23	05.39	18.05
14th	11.33	–	06.31	18.53
15th	00.01	12.10	07.13	19.33
16th	00.33	12.45	07.47	20.05 *
17th	01.04	13.19	08.15	20.33 *
18th	01.35	13.49	08.41	21.00
19th	02.02	14.14	09.08	21.29
20th	02.25	14.36	09.38	22.00
21st	02.47	15.04	10.10	22.31
22nd	03.18	15.40	10.43	23.06
23rd	03.58	16.25	11.22	23.49
24th	04.51	17.27	–	12.11
25th	06.18	19.07	00.49	13.26
26th	08.07	20.32	02.25	15.05
27th	09.12	21.36	03.48	16.18
28th	10.08	22.31	04.54	17.21
29th	10.58	23.21	05.55	18.20
30th	11.44	00.07	06.54	19.18
31st	12.29	00.51	07.49	20.12

A

THE SKY AT NIGHT

Moon phases

New moon – 1st August

1st quarter – 7th August

Full moon – 15th August

3rd quarter – 23rd August

New moon – 30th August

In the night sky this month

10th	Close approach of the moon and Jupiter, first visible in the twilight around 20.00 at about 16 degrees above the southern horizon. They set at 00.30 in the southwest.
12th	Close approach of the moon and Saturn, which appear as dusk falls at about 21.00 at 12 degrees above the south/southeastern horizon. They reach 16 degrees in the south at 22.00 before setting in the southwest at about 02.00.
12th, 13th	Perseids meteor shower.

Moon rise and set

	Inverness		Padstow		
	Rise	Set	Rise	Set	
1st	05.11	22.06	05.50	21.39	new moon
2nd	06.42	22.30	07.12	22.13	
3rd	08.16	22.50	08.37	22.41	
4th	09.49	23.06	10.00	23.06	
5th	11.19	23.21	11.21	23.29	
6th	12.47	23.37	12.40	23.52	
7th	14.12	23.54	13.57	–	1st quarter
8th	15.35	–	15.12	00.17	
9th	16.53	00.14	16.23	00.45	
10th	18.06	00.40	17.29	01.18	
11th	19.08	01.14	18.28	01.57	
12th	19.58	01.59	19.19	02.44	
13th	20.36	02.54	20.01	03.38	
14th	21.04	03.58	20.35	04.38	
15th	21.26	05.07	21.03	05.41	full moon
16th	21.43	06.19	21.27	06.45	
17th	21.56	07.31	21.47	07.50	
18th	22.09	08.43	22.06	08.55	
19th	22.20	09.55	22.24	10.00	
20th	22.32	11.07	22.43	11.05	
21st	22.46	12.20	23.03	12.11	
22nd	23.02	13.35	23.26	13.19	
23rd	23.22	14.52	23.54	14.28	3rd quarter
24th	23.50	16.09	–	15.38	
25th	–	17.23	00.29	16.46	
26th	00.30	18.29	01.14	17.50	
27th	01.26	19.22	02.11	18.45	
28th	02.39	20.01	03.21	19.31	
29th	04.06	20.30	04.40	20.08	
30th	05.40	20.52	06.05	20.39	new moon
31st	07.15	21.10	07.31	21.05	

A

Meteor shower of the month – the Perseids

As the earth passes through the debris left behind by Comet Swift-Tuttle, we get one of the most impressive and reliable meteor showers of the year, the Perseids. This year the peak of the show on the 12th and 13th coincides with an almost full moon, so conditions aren't perfect. The best time for viewing is from midnight to 04.00; the radiant will be at about 40 degrees above the horizon in the northeast, and the moon will set at around 03.24 on the 13th. Even if you aren't up so late, the Perseids are so bright and plentiful that if you look in the evening you should catch them anyway. The trails will be more numerous just before dawn but earlier in the evening they are more elongated as the dust particles graze the atmosphere at an angle. Comet Swift-Tuttle was identified when it passed earth in 1862, and it led to Italian astronomer Giovanni Virginio Schiaparelli discovering the link between comets and meteor showers in 1866. It last passed by in 1992 before heading off again on its 133-year orbit.

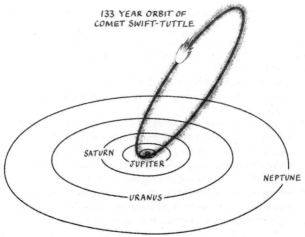

133 YEAR ORBIT OF COMET SWIFT-TUTTLE

SATURN
JUPITER
NEPTUNE
URANUS

THE GARDEN

Planting by the moon

New moon to 1st quarter: 1st–7th. Sow crops that develop below ground. Dig the soil.

1st quarter to full moon: 7th–15th. Sow crops that develop above ground. Plant seedlings and young plants.

Full moon to 3rd quarter: 15th–23rd. Harvest crops for immediate eating. Harvest fruit.

3rd quarter to new moon: 23rd–30th. Prune. Harvest for storage. Fertilise and mulch the soil.

Job of the month – trim lavender and other herbs

Lavender has finished flowering now, so shear off all of the flowers and just a little of this year's growth. This will encourage it to grow bushy and keep a nice shape. This is a good moment to prune other herbs such as sage, rosemary, thyme and oregano, as it will stimulate them to put on a new flush of fresh, tempting leaves before the weather cools.

Glut of the month – loganberries and autumn raspberries

Loganberries and raspberries provide a wonderful late-summer treat. Loganberries turn deep red or purple when ripe, raspberries vibrant red. They will not keep, so eat quickly or turn them into jam.

- **Peach melba:** Blend berries with a little lime juice and icing sugar, then sieve to make a vibrant sauce for pouring over peaches and ice cream.
- **Raspberry or loganberry vinegar:** This is a brilliantly useful ingredient for salad dressings and for deglazing pans for sauces. Fill a jar with 500g raspberries or loganberries and 1 litre white wine vinegar. Seal and leave for a month in a cool, dark place before decanting into bottles.
- **Frozen berries:** Freeze berries in a single layer on a tray and then bundle them up in a bag. Drop the frozen berries onto yoghurt or eat them as frozen fruit treats on hot days.

A

Flower of the month – sunflower

Latin name: *Helianthus annuus* (from the Greek *helios*, meaning 'sun' and *anthos*, meaning 'flower'; *annuus* is Latin for 'annual' or 'lives for one year').
Common name: sunflower.

Walk through the gates of any allotment site in August and your path will be lined with sunflowers: sunny, bold and bright. The first you notice will be the giants – those that were sown by pudgy-fingered toddlers into yoghurt pots of soil back in spring and now boast massive yolk-yellow discs atop metres of stem – but then you will spot the myriad other shades of sun and sunset, and the multi-stemmed types for bunches and vases, every one of them looking like August in flower form. Sunflowers are beautiful anywhere but they particularly suit summer in the city, their best backdrop not the well-sheared yew hedge, but the red brick wall.

Not only do they look like the sun but they love it, too. They will grow and flower at their best when grown in the sunniest possible spot, but their young leaves and buds also exhibit phototropism, following the sun across the sky from east to west each day, before travelling back across to the east each night to await the dawning sun. They are annuals, so if you want these bright and funky pollen-heavy flowers buzzing with grateful insects on your plot every August, you will have to make like the toddlers and sow them indoors in spring.

NATURE

Inside the beehive in August

Come August there are suddenly fewer flowers, and the foraging is leaner. The height of summer has passed and plants have moved into a new phase: they have been pollinated and their own task is now fruiting and setting seed rather than flowering. The bees continue to work the gardens and hedgerows anyway to keep nectar and pollen flowing into the hive, albeit far less bountifully than last month. Moorland areas are the exception, as heather starts to flower now, producing a very distinctive honey: dark reddish amber in colour and strong, tangy and woody in flavour. Summer honey is taken this month – the 'supers' (boxes of frames to be filled with honeycomb) are removed, the wax cappings sliced off the honeycomb with a hot knife to reveal the liquid honey within, and the combs spun in an extractor to pull out the honey and decant it into golden jars.

Look out for...the grasshopper chorus

The sound you can hear as you swish through long late-summer grass, that pulsing chik-chik-chik, is grasshoppers doing things their own way. Most mating rituals occurred in spring – with the unarguable logic that the earlier you get your babies born, the stronger they'll be to survive the following winter – but grasshoppers mate in late summer, laying the fertilised eggs into dry ground to hatch next spring. Stridulation, the act of rubbing a row of pegs on their back legs against their forewings, acts as a mating call, and is the sound of late summer.

A

THE KITCHEN

Cheese of the month – Old Demdike

Old Demdike is a semi-hard, washed-rind ewes' cheese from Somerset, and is only made between the spring and autumn equinoxes. Cheese maker Homewood Cheeses uses milk from local flocks that produce between November and September, but the earliest milk is 'thin' and better suited to other types of cheese making. The milk that comes after March, when the ewes are mid-lactation and out feeding on grass, is fuller. It has a higher proportion of fats and milk solids, and is better suited to the production of moist, sweet and delicate Old Demdike. Ambient temperature is important, too: warmer nights allow the curds to settle naturally, which is essential for developing the distinctive creamy, semi-hard texture. It is sufficiently ripened at around eight weeks and will happily mature for another eight, so will be around into autumn, but the best batches from early and mid-summer are to be had now.

In season

The first **figs** and **melons** start to ripen this month. **Plums** are at their best. Summer-fruiting **raspberries** finish now but autumn-fruiting varieties pick up the baton. Other fruits in season include **blackcurrants, redcurrants, tayberries, apricots, peaches, blueberries**, early ripening **apples** and **pears**.

The **tomatoes** are coming, along with other Mediterranean vegetables: **sweet peppers, chilli peppers** and **aubergines** join **sweetcorn, courgettes, carrots, fennel, French** and **runner beans, potatoes, beetroot, lettuce, sorrel, spinach, cucumbers** and **radish. Herbs** are plentiful.

Look out for **cobnuts**, a type of hazelnut, picked when green, unripe and crunchy. In the hedgerows **crab apples** and **elderberries** are just starting to ripen. **Sea buckthorn** is fruiting.

Plaice, mackerel, sardines, megrim sole, squid, crab, lobster and **scallops** are all in season.

Goat meat is available all year round, but it is particularly good and cheap this month, as increased production is timed to coincide with carnival season and with Eid al-Adha.

RECIPES

Tourlou tourlou

The name for this dish means something along the lines of 'all mixed up' and it is in the marvellous Greek tradition of slow-cooking vegetables with lots of olive oil and then eating them just warm, with bread and cheese. It is designed for this wonderful moment on the vegetable patch, when all of the most flavourful Mediterranean vegetables have started producing in earnest, joining the stalwart courgettes and potatoes that have been going for a while. If you can make this dish entirely from your plot, then you should be very proud of yourself.

Serves 4
Ingredients
7 beefsteak tomatoes
2 medium potatoes, peeled
1 aubergine
2 courgettes
1 onion
6 cloves garlic
A handful each of basil, mint and oregano
240ml extra virgin olive oil
Salt and pepper

A

Method

Preheat your oven to 190°C, Gas Mark 5. Boil a kettle full of water. Take 3 of the tomatoes and cut a cross in their skin at the base, then place them in a bowl and pour over the just boiled water. About 10 minutes later, remove the tomatoes and the skin should peel away easily. Put them into a bowl and mash them, then add 120ml water and mix in. Set aside.

Slice the potatoes, the rest of the tomatoes, aubergine and courgettes into 1cm rounds, then thinly slice the onion and garlic. Finely chop all of the herbs. Coat the bottom of a large roasting tin with some of the olive oil, then start layering the vegetables. First put in all of the potatoes, then a scattering of garlic, half the onions, half the tomato rounds, some salt and pepper, and a handful of herbs. Next add all of the aubergine slices and half of the remaining garlic, onions, herbs and oil, plus more salt and pepper. Finally, add all of the courgette slices, the rest of the tomato rounds, garlic, onion, herbs and oil, and some more salt and pepper. Top with the crushed tomato and water mixture.

Bake, uncovered, for 1 hour, then turn the vegetables and return to the oven. Do this every 20 minutes until all the vegetables are cooked through, at least another hour. You can serve this immediately but it is even better the next day when the flavours have had time to marry. Eat it with feta cheese and hunks of bread to soak up the juices.

Blackberry and honey cake for Lughnasadh

Celebrate summer's bounty with this soft, fragrant cake. It is quite pudding-like, because of the fresh fruit, and really needs to be eaten the day it is made, ideally still warm with whipped double cream. Use this year's local honey if you can find it.

Ingredients

100g caster sugar
150g softened butter
Grated zest of 1 lemon
1 vanilla pod
2 eggs

2 tablespoons runny honey (if you only have set honey, then warm it so that it is spoonable)

100g self-raising flour

50g ground almonds

1 teaspoon baking powder

100g blackberries

Method

Preheat the oven to 190°C, Gas Mark 5 and grease and line a 20cm cake tin. Beat together the caster sugar, butter, zest and the seeds from the vanilla pod until light and fluffy, then add one egg at a time, beating well in between so that each becomes well incorporated before adding the next. Add the honey and beat that in, too, then add the flour, ground almonds, baking powder and blackberries. Fold them together gently, until everything is wet. Tip into the cake tin and smooth the surface. Bake for about 45–50 minutes, or until a toothpick pushed into the centre of the cake comes out clean. Remove from the oven and leave to stand for 10 minutes before removing from the tin and placing on a rack to cool further. Serve just warm.

A

Cherry shandy

Here's another way to enjoy the grains and the fruit of the moment, if cake isn't your thing. Once made, the cherry slush can be used a few ways: in a shandy, as here, or as a sort of rough and ready cherryade with fizzy water, or with ice and a measure of Kirsch.

Makes 6–8 shandies

Ingredients
300ml water
300g sugar
500g cherries, stoned
Juice of 1 lemon
A few drops almond essence
Pale ale

Method

Put the water and the sugar into a saucepan and heat, stirring, to dissolve, then simmer for a minute or so. Remove from the heat and leave to cool. Put the stoned cherries into a food processor or blender and whizz until they are smooth. Tip them into the cooled syrup with the lemon juice and the almond essence. Stir, bottle and chill until needed. Fill about a third of a glass with the cherry liquid, top up with the pale ale, and serve immediately.

CEREALS

A

A SONG FOR HARVEST

'John Barleycorn'
Traditional

This apparently macabre song is really a celebration of John Barleycorn, the personification of the barley crop. Despite his terrible treatment at the hands of the men who see to him – throwing clods upon his head, cutting him at the knee, grinding him between stones – none of them can do without him, and he proves the strongest of them all, presumably seeing them off in the form of beer and whisky.

There were three men came out o' the west, their for - tunes for to try, And these three men made a sol - emn vow John Bar - ley - corn must die, They ploughed, and sowed, and harrowed him in, threw clods up on his head, And these three men made a sol - emn vow John Barley - corn was dead.

They let him lie for a very long time
Till the rains from heaven did fall
And little Sir John sprung up his head
And so amazed them all.

They let him stand for a long time,
Till he looked both pale and wan,
And little Sir John grew a long, long beard
And so become a man.

They let him stand for a long time
Till he looked both pale and wan
And little Sir John grew a long, long beard
And so become a man.

They hired men with the scythes so sharp
To cut him off at the knee;
They rolled him and tied him by the waist –
Serving him most barbarously.

They hired men with their crab-tree sticks
To cut him skin from bone
And the miller he served him worse than that
For he ground him between two stones.

Here's little Sir John in the nut brown bowl
And brandy in the glass
And little Sir John in the nut brown bowl
Proved the strongest man at last.

The huntsman he can't hunt the fox
Nor so loudly to blow his horn
And the tinker he can't mend kettle nor pots
Without little Lord Barleycorn.

A

September

The naming of September

Sultain (Scots Gaelic)
September (Scots/Ulster Scots)
Meán Fómhair (Irish Gaelic)
Mean-fouyir (Manx)
Medi (Welsh)
Gwynngala (Cornish)
Septembre (Jèrriais)

September was the Roman name for this month, which means 'seventh month', dating from the time when March was the start of the year. The English names for the months follow this pattern for the rest of the year, October being the eighth month, November the ninth and December the tenth. Most of the languages of the British Isles take a more agricultural approach to September. Meán Fómhair in Irish Gaelic means 'mid' and 'harvest', and is echoed in the Manx Mean-fouyir, while the Welsh Medi means 'harvest' or 'reaping'. As often, the Cornish name for the month – Gwynngala – arises from Breton rather than from any of the languages of the British Isles. In Breton, September is *Gwengolo*, which may come from *gwenn* meaning 'white', and *kolo* meaning 'straw', a reference to crops ripening and stems blanching in the sun. The Scots Gaelic Sultain is from a word that means 'pleasing, pleasant, fat': there are good times and feasting to be had as the harvest comes in.

A HINDU TALE FOR SEPTEMBER

Ganesh and the moon

The benevolent, wise, elephant-headed god Ganesh had a
terrible sweet tooth. One year on his birthday his devotees
plied him with his favourite sweet: modak, a delicious
coconut- and jaggery-filled dumpling. Ganesh could not
resist: he ate and ate until his belly was even fuller and
rounder than it normally was, and that was going some.
Finally, he waddled off slowly through the night, with more
modak gathered up in his clothes. Now in these days the
moon shone full and bright all month long, but despite his
way being well lit, he tripped and fell, tearing his clothes and
scattering the sweets everywhere. The moon, who was vain
and regarded himself as very handsome, had always thought
Ganesh looked funny with his little short legs and his big
belly. When the moon saw Ganesh looking so undignified, he
fell about laughing and tears ran down his face, and this sent
the usually gentle Ganesh into a rage. 'How dare you laugh at
me?!' he bellowed. 'You think you are so beautiful! I curse you
to disappear from the sky and never show your face again!'
The moon was mortified: no one would ever see his handsome
face again? He begged Ganesh for mercy and Ganesh quickly
softened, but he knew that he could not take back his curse
completely. 'There will be only one day each month when you
vanish from the sky, and after that day you will grow until you
reach your full size, then shrink back to nothing again,' he
declared. And that is why the moon waxes and wanes.

Ganesh's birthday celebration, Ganesh Chaturthi, is held
on the fourth day of the Hindu month Bhadrapada, which
this year falls on 2nd September. It is celebrated with prayers,
worship, processions and, of course, many sweets. Ganesh is
widely revered as the remover of obstacles, and as the god of
new beginnings and projects, making him the perfect patron
for September.

S

WEATHER

Hurricane season

It is hurricane season in the West Indies, which runs from 1st June to 30th November and peaks on 10th September, and this can send strong winds and heavy rainfall wheeling across the Atlantic, resulting in autumn storms for the UK and Ireland. For several hundred years a hurricane was named after the saint's day it fell on, and then from the 1950s to the 1970s hurricanes were given women's names. Now there are six lists – each containing alternating male and female names – that we cycle through, with some names retired and replaced if they have been attached to a particularly strong or damaging hurricane. This year's potential crop are: Andrea, Barry, Chantal, Dean, Erin, Fernand, Gabrielle, Humberto, Imelda, Jerry, Karen, Lorenzo, Melissa, Nestor, Olga, Pablo, Rebekah, Sebastien, Tanya, Van and Wendy. A calm season would stop at Imelda, and it would be rare to get beyond Melissa.

Average temperatures (°C):	Inverness 12, Padstow 14
Average sunshine hours per day:	Inverness 4, Padstow 5
Average days of rainfall:	Inverness 17, Padstow 19
Average rainfall total (mm):	Inverness 30, Padstow 67

Day length

During the course of September, day length decreases by:

2 hours 21 minutes (to 11 hours 37 minutes) – Inverness
1 hour 48 minutes (to 11 hours 43 minutes) – Padstow

Autumnal equinox is on Monday 23rd September 2019, at 08.50. The sun reaches an altitude of 38 degrees at midday.

Sunrise and set

	Inverness		Padstow	
	Rise	Set	Rise	Set
1st	06.17	20.15	06.33	20.05
2nd	06.19	20.12	06.34	20.03
3rd	06.21	20.09	06.36	20.00
4th	06.23	20.07	06.37	19.58
5th	06.25	20.04	06.39	19.56
6th	06.27	20.01	06.40	19.54
7th	06.29	19.58	06.42	19.52
8th	06.31	19.56	06.44	19.49
9th	06.33	19.53	06.45	19.47
10th	06.36	19.50	06.47	19.45
11th	06.38	19.47	06.48	19.43
12th	06.40	19.45	06.50	19.41
13th	06.42	19.42	06.51	19.38
14th	06.44	19.39	06.53	19.36
15th	06.46	19.36	06.54	19.34
16th	06.48	19.33	06.56	19.32
17th	06.50	19.31	06.57	19.29
18th	06.52	19.28	06.59	19.27
19th	06.54	19.25	07.00	19.25
20th	06.56	19.22	07.02	19.23
21st	06.58	19.19	07.03	19.20
22nd	07.00	19.17	07.05	19.18
23rd	07.03	19.14	07.06	19.16
24th	07.05	19.11	07.08	19.14
25th	07.07	19.08	07.10	19.12
26th	07.09	19.06	07.11	19.09
27th	07.11	19.03	07.13	19.07
28th	07.13	19.00	07.14	19.05
29th	07.15	18.57	07.16	19.03
30th	07.17	18.54	07.17	19.00

S

THE SEA

Average sea temperature

Isle of Lewis:	13.1°C
Whitby:	14.9°C
Belfast:	14.2°C
Cork:	15.7°C
Swansea:	16.5°C
Brighton:	17.3°C
Falmouth:	16.3°C

Spring and neap tides

The spring tides are the most extreme tides of the month, with the highest rises and falls, and the neap tides are the least extreme, with the smallest. Exact timings vary around the coast, but expect them around the following dates:

Spring tides: 1st–2nd, 15th–16th, and 29th–30th

Neap tides: 7th–8th and 23rd–24th

In the tide timetable opposite, spring tides are shown with an asterisk.

September tide timetable for Dover

For your local high tide differences on Dover, see page 8.

	High water		*Low water*	
	Morning	Afternoon	Morning	Afternoon
1st	–	13.12	08.37	20.59 *
2nd	01.34	13.56	09.18	21.41 *
3rd	02.17	14.40	09.55	22.19
4th	03.02	15.26	10.31	22.57
5th	03.50	16.14	11.09	23.37
6th	04.43	17.09	11.52	–
7th	05.44	18.13	00.26	12.49
8th	06.57	19.35	01.30	14.06
9th	08.25	21.21	02.47	15.28
10th	09.42	22.25	04.06	16.48
11th	10.34	23.09	05.19	17.49
12th	11.13	23.43	06.10	18.34
13th	11.48	–	06.49	19.10
14th	00.11	12.20	07.21	19.39
15th	00.37	12.50	07.47	20.05 *
16th	01.04	13.17	08.13	20.32 *
17th	01.28	13.39	08.41	21.01
18th	01.49	14.02	09.11	21.31
19th	02.13	14.30	09.42	22.01
20th	02.44	15.05	10.14	22.34
21st	03.24	15.49	10.51	23.15
22nd	04.15	16.48	11.39	–
23rd	05.33	18.50	00.11	12.48
24th	07.47	20.21	01.44	14.36
25th	08.56	21.25	03.26	15.57
26th	09.53	22.20	04.37	17.03
27th	10.42	23.08	05.39	18.04
28th	11.27	23.52	06.37	19.01
29th	–	12.10	07.28	19.52 *
30th	00.33	12.52	08.14	20.37 *

S

THE SKY AT NIGHT

Moon phases

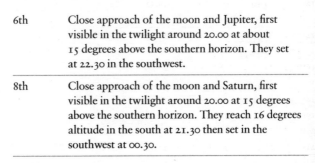

1st quarter – 6th September

Full moon – 14th September

3rd quarter – 22nd September

New moon – 28th September

In the night sky this month

6th	Close approach of the moon and Jupiter, first visible in the twilight around 20.00 at about 15 degrees above the southern horizon. They set at 22.30 in the southwest.
8th	Close approach of the moon and Saturn, first visible in the twilight around 20.00 at 15 degrees above the southern horizon. They reach 16 degrees altitude in the south at 21.30 then set in the southwest at 00.30.

Moon rise and set

	Inverness		*Padstow*		
	Rise	Set	Rise	Set	
1st	08.50	21.26	08.56	21.30	
2nd	10.22	21.41	10.19	21.54	
3rd	11.52	21.58	11.40	22.18	
4th	13.19	22.18	12.58	22.46	
5th	14.41	22.42	14.13	23.18	
6th	15.57	23.13	15.22	23.55	1st quarter
7th	17.04	23.55	16.24	–	
8th	17.57	–	17.18	00.40	
9th	18.39	00.47	18.02	01.32	
10th	19.09	01.48	18.38	02.30	
11th	19.32	02.56	19.07	03.32	
12th	19.50	04.08	19.32	04.37	
13th	20.04	05.20	19.53	05.42	
14th	20.17	06.32	20.12	06.47	full moon
15th	20.28	07.44	20.30	07.52	
16th	20.40	08.57	20.49	08.57	
17th	20.52	10.10	21.08	10.03	
18th	21.07	11.24	21.30	11.10	
19th	21.25	12.40	21.55	12.18	
20th	21.49	13.56	22.26	13.27	
21st	22.23	15.10	23.06	14.34	
22nd	23.10	16.18	23.56	15.38	3rd quarter
23rd	–	17.14	–	16.35	
24th	00.14	17.58	00.58	17.23	
25th	01.33	18.30	02.12	18.03	
26th	03.02	18.54	03.32	18.36	
27th	04.36	19.13	04.57	19.04	
28th	06.12	19.29	06.23	19.28	new moon
29th	07.47	19.44	07.48	19.52	
30th	09.20	20.00	09.13	20.17	

S

THE GARDEN

Planting by the moon

New moon to 1st quarter: 1st–6th. Sow crops that develop below ground. Dig the soil.

1st quarter to full moon: 6th–14th. Sow crops that develop above ground. Plant seedlings and young plants.

Full moon to 3rd quarter: 14th–22nd. Harvest crops for immediate eating. Harvest fruit.

3rd quarter to new moon: 22nd–28th. Prune. Harvest for storage. Fertilise and mulch the soil.

Jobs of the month – sow hardy seed for next year

Get seeds into the ground while it is still warm and you will have an earlier and better display of flowers next year. Hardy annuals for cutting such as calendula, cornflower, larkspur, love-in-a-mist and scabious can be sown in rows directly where they are to flower and thinned out later. This is also a great moment for sowing meadows (or small patches of meadow).

Glut of the month – figs

The hardiest fig, 'Brown Turkey', grows brilliantly in the British Isles, and on golden September days, while sitting under a laden tree, we can fool ourselves that our climate really isn't so bad after all. Figs must be a bruise purple, yielding to the touch, and ideally sun-warmed before you eat them.

- **An easy tart Tatin:** Put a circle of baking parchment in the base of a cake tin and dot with butter, honey and cinnamon. Fill with halved figs, cut side down, and tuck a circle of puff pastry over them. Bake at 180°c, Gas Mark 4 until the pastry is crisp and browned. Turn out from the tin, remove the paper, drizzle with more honey and serve with ice cream.
- **Grilled figs:** Cut a cross in the top of several figs and place the figs in an ovenproof dish. Push in a knob of butter

then drizzle with honey and sprinkle with thyme. Grill for 5 minutes, then serve the figs with their juices and some toasted pine nuts on Greek yoghurt.

- **Figs with ham and walnuts:** Serve figs on a plate with Serrano ham and toasted walnuts.

Flower of the month – Michaelmas daisy

Latin name: *Aster amellus* (*Aster*, from the Greek for 'star'; *amellus*, origin uncertain – either meaning 'from the river Mella' (*a-mella*) in northern Italy, or referring to the fact that the plant is supposed to cure sick bees, which produce 'no honey', or '*a-mel*').

Common names: aster, Italian aster, Michaelmas daisy.

The Michaelmas daisy is called this because it is dependably in flower on the Feast of the Archangel Michael: Michaelmas Day, the 29th September. A traditional rhyme goes: 'The Michaelmas daisies, among dead weeds,/Bloom for St Michael's valorous deeds.' It is no mean feat, for, as the rhyme points out, most flowers have packed it in by now. But asters come along late in the year with colour and pollen galore, their fuzz of yellow-centred purple daisy flowers proving hugely useful to gardeners, bees, butterflies and moths alike. This is the time both to choose asters and to plant them: get them and other herbaceous perennials into the warm earth now, and let the autumn rains loosen and draw out their roots. The plants will be strong next year. Michaelmas has always been associated with the harvest and with a wrapping up of the agricultural year, and in the language of flowers the Michaelmas daisy symbolises a departure or farewell. In the garden it certainly heralds the beginning of the end of summer.

NATURE

Inside the beehive in September

In September the colony shrinks in size as the female worker bees reach the ends of their natural lives and are not replaced in such great number. The male drones are no longer needed and will use up precious winter supplies, so they are harshly ousted from the hive and left to die. Natural sources of food for the bees become scarce, but gardens planted with late summer flowers step into the gap, as does Himalayan balsam, an invasive and ecologically damaging plant of waterways, but a good source of late nectar. Wasps can become pests as they are ousted from their own nests and seek the sweet rewards they have been used to receiving from their own queen, so they may attack hives for honey. The bees shore up gaps in the hive and reduce the size of the hive entrance with propolis (resin collected by the bees from tree buds, mixed with beeswax and their saliva).

Look out for...daddy-longlegs

Here they come every September, lolloping drunkenly along and bashing off of windows, ceilings and – uh! – faces. This is the month of the daddy-longlegs, more correctly known as crane flies. The larvae (known as leatherjackets) have spent the summer below grass, munching on roots and decaying plant matter. Autumn rains loosen the soil and signal that it is time to hatch, and the daddy-longlegs rise haphazardly into the air. They will live for a maximum of two weeks, mating and laying, and providing a rich source of food for birds heading into winter.

THE KITCHEN

Cheese of the month – Mont d'Or/Winslade

September brings with it one of the events of the cheese year: the release of the Vacherin Mont d'Or, and its arrival in British cheesemongers. Mont d'Or is made in Switzerland and France from the milk of Simmental cows when they come down from the high summertime mountain pastures in the Mont d'Or massif on the border of the two countries. In the summer their milk is used for Comté and Gruyère, but indoors in winter – and fed entirely on hay – they produce less milk, and it is fattier, so production switches. Mont d'Or is a nutty, smelly, unctuous cheese matured in a spruce collar, which gives it resinous notes. It can only be produced between 15th August and 15th March and is released onto the international market in September.

British cheesemakers Hampshire Cheeses produce their own spruce-matured Mont d'Or-style cheese, Winslade, but it is made all year round. It has a gentler flavour and more floral notes – somewhere between a Mont d'Or and a Camembert.

In season

Mediterranean vegetables are at their best now: **tomatoes** and **aubergines** are reaching their brief and delicious glut, and **chillies** are ready for picking. **Runner beans, French beans, cucumbers, sweetcorn, beetroot, broccoli, carrots, salad leaves, maincrop potatoes,** and more are in full flow too. **Leeks, kale, turnips,** and other autumn/winter crops are starting to come in.

Fruits of the month include **plums, blackberries, apples, pears** and autumn **raspberries**. **Figs** are now ripe and juicy, and there are plenty of **melons, nectarines** and **peaches** to be had.

In the hedgerow look for **damsons, elderberries** and the last of the **blackberries**. **Cobnuts** and **hazelnuts** are plentiful.

There are still lots of fresh herbs around, including **parsley, oregano, thyme, basil** and **coriander**.

Grouse, partridge, duck, goose and **guinea fowl** are coming in to season.

Crab, scallops, lobster, hake, megrim sole, sardines, mackerel, scallops and **plaice** are all abundant.

S

RECIPES

A Michaelmas salad

Michaelmas Day, 29th September, used to be called Crack-Nut Day. Hazelnuts were cracked and eaten in church, apparently with such gusto that the service would be drowned out.

Serves 4
Ingredients
For the dressing
50g blackberries
1 teaspoon runny honey
1 tablespoon cider vinegar
3 tablespoons extra virgin olive oil
Salt and pepper
For the salad
50g rocket
50g watercress
6 ripe figs, quartered
150g blackberries
125g seasonal cheese – soft ripened cheese such as Winsdale or a fresh goats' cheese
50g hazelnuts, toasted and very roughly chopped

Method

To make the dressing, pound the blackberries in a pestle and mortar. Add the other dressing ingredients and pound together.

To assemble the salad, arrange the rocket and watercress on the plates and top with the figs, blackberries, cheese (each portion chopped into a few pieces) and hazelnuts. Drizzle over the dressing and serve.

Sweet dosa with jaggery and coconut – Vela dosa

These are not Ganesh's favourite modak but they do contain many of the same ingredients. Jaggery is unrefined cane sugar juice, reduced to a paste and left to dry. It is fairly easy to find in Indian shops or in supermarket international aisles, but if you can't find it, use muscovado sugar, which has some similar complex caramel flavours. It is sweeter so use a little less.

Makes about 8 small dosas
Ingredients
3 tablespoons desiccated coconut
Juice of half a lime
100g shaved jaggery (or 75g muscovado sugar)
4 cardamom pods
70g plain flour
70g rice flour
30g cashew nuts, chopped
30g raisins
Ghee or clarified butter, for frying
Banana, sliced, to serve (optional)

Method

Start by reconstituting the coconut. Put it in a bowl and add the lime juice and 5 tablespoons boiling water. Mix, cover and leave for at least 10 minutes or until most of the water is absorbed. In a small pan heat 120ml water with the jaggery (or muscovado sugar) until it dissolves, sieve it to remove any impurities and let it cool. Use a pestle and mortar to lightly bash the cardamom pods until they crack, remove the pods, and release the seeds into the mortar before pounding them to powder.

To make the batter, put the plain flour, rice flour, coconut, jaggery water, cardamom seeds, cashew nuts and raisins into a large bowl and mix well. You can use the batter immediately but it is best left for a few hours, or even until the next day. To fry the dosas, heat a frying pan and add a little ghee, turning the heat to low once it has melted. Using a ladle, stir the mixture to be sure to take up some pieces of raisin and nut, then pour half a ladleful into the frying pan and spread it out a little, using the back of the ladle in a circular motion. Once the edges of the dosa start to lift, flip it over and cook the other side, adding more ghee if you like. Repeat for the remainder, keeping the dosas warm in the oven until all are ready. Serve on their own or with some sliced banana.

Damson vodka

Any hedgerow fruit will make a beautiful fruity, syrupy liqueur for Christmas – here I have used damsons. You will need a 2-litre preserving jar.

Makes 1.25 litres
Ingredients
450g damsons
225g caster sugar
1 litre vodka

Method

Put the damsons into the preserving jar and pour in the sugar and vodka. Seal and shake, then store somewhere dark and cool. Shake the jar once a week. It will be drinkable after a month, but better after three. Real aficionados will open theirs not this Christmas coming, but the following Christmas, when it will be luxuriously syrupy. Strain off the fruits and bottle.

HEDGEROW FRUITS

A SONG FOR MICHAELMAS

'The Nutting Girl'
Traditional

Nuts were once an essential source of free food for poor rural families, and teenagers would be sent off into the woods during nutting season to gather what they could. With predictable results. Nutting became a byword for saucier pursuits, leading to the once-common phrase 'a good year for nuts, a good year for babies'.

Now come all you jo-vial fel-lows, come lis-ten to my song.

is a lit-tle di-tty and it won't de-tain you long. It's of a fair you

dam-sel, oh she lived down in Kent, a rose one sum-mer's mor ning, and

she a-nut-ting went. With a fal-lal to my ral-tal-lal

Whack-fol-the-dear-ol-day, And what few nuts that

poor girl had, she threw them all a-way.

It's of a brisk young farmer, was a-ploughing of his land,
He called unto his horses, and bid them gently stand.
As he sat down upon his plough, all for a song to sing,
His voice was so melodious, it made the valleys ring.

> *Chorus:*
> *With a fal-lal to my ral-tal-lal*
> *Whack-fol-the-dear-ol-day*
> *And what few nuts that poor girl had*
> *She threw them all away.*

It's of this fair young damsel, she was nutting in the wood,
His voice was so melodious, it charmed her as she stood.
In that lonely wood, she could no longer stay,
And what few nuts she had, poor girl, she threw them all away.

> *Chorus*

She then came to young Johnny, as he sat on his plough,
Said she, 'Young man, I really feel I cannot tell you how.'
He took her to some shady broom and there he laid her down,
Said she, 'Young man, I think I feel the world go round and
round.'

> *Chorus*

So come all you young women, take warning by my song
If you should a-nutting go, don't stay from home too long.
For if you should stay too late, to hear the ploughboy sing,
You might have a young farmer to nurse up in the spring.

> *Chorus*

S

October

1   End of Rosh Hashanah – Jewish New Year, (Jewish)

8   End of Navaratri – autumn festival (Hindu)

9   Yom Kippur – Day of Atonement (Jewish) – festivities begin at sundown on 8th

14   First Day of Tabernacles/Sukkot (Jewish)

21   Apple Day

27   Diwali – Festival of Lights (Hindu/Sikh/Jain)

27   British Summer Time ends. Clocks go back one hour at 02.00

28   October bank holiday, Republic of Ireland

31   Hallowe'en

The naming of October

Dàmhair (Scots Gaelic)
October (Scots/Ulster Scots)
Deireadh Fómhair (Irish Gaelic)
Jerry-fouyir (Manx)
Hydref (Welsh)
Hedra (Cornish)
Octobre (Jèrriais)

The naming of this month in the languages of the British Isles gives glimpses into past autumnal concerns. Two are clear-cut: Deireadh Fómhair (Irish Gaelic) and Jerry-fouyir (Manx) both contain words meaning 'end' and 'harvest' – it is the final chance to gather in crops. But the Welsh Hydref (which is the Welsh word for both 'autumn' and 'October') is thought to be derived from *hydd* meaning 'stag' and *bref* meaning 'lowing, bleating', and the Cornish Hedra appears to come from the same root. The Scots Gaelic Dàmhair similarly points to the importance of deer in this month, and comes from *damh*, meaning 'rut'. It is rutting time, when the stags' bellows are heard at dawn and dusk – and the start of hunting season.

A WELSH FOLK TALE FOR OCTOBER

Merlin's apples

There are many real-world candidates for the legendary Isle of Apples of Arthurian legend, widely known as the Isle of Avalon (derived from *afal*, Welsh for 'apple'). One such is Ynys Enlli, or Bardsey Island, off the tip of the Llŷn Peninsula in Gwynned, Wales. Here it is said that the wizard Merlin lived in a magical glass castle, and Morgan le Fay – the healer and enchantress, and King Arthur's half-sister – studied under him. Apples often play a magical role in folk tales and myths, the trees being gateways to fairy lands or the underworld, and the apples themselves poisoned or enchanted. Avalon was one such gateway, and the trees on its slopes produced fruit all year round. Morgan brought Arthur to Avalon when he was mortally wounded, and he was either laid to rest, or – in keeping with the apple island's powers – he still awaits the moment for his messianic return, to claim the throne.

In 1998 a keen ornithologist, Andy Clarke, was on Bardsey Island to catch and ring birds. Needing bait for his net, he collected some windfall apples under a gnarled tree in the lee of an old house. He noticed that, unusually for north Wales, the apples were disease-free, so he sent samples to the National Fruit Collection at Brogdale in Kent. They pronounced them unique: no one had seen this apple before. Cuttings were taken and Bardsey Island Apple Trees can now be bought, in small quantities. The apple is rosy in colour and tastes lemony and sweet; it cooks to a light golden fluff. Locals say that the tree has always been there, and they know the apples as 'Merlin's apples'. There is a theory that the myth of the glass castle arose from some kind of early greenhouse that allowed apples to thrive in Bardsey's harsh conditions.

Apple Day falls on 21st October. Started in 1990 by the charity Common Ground, it was created as an opportunity to celebrate the rich history and variety of apples in the British Isles. Look out for local orchard events.

O

WEATHER

First frosts

First frosts are coming, tuck up your tender plants. Indeed for a few in the Highlands of Scotland they could have already hit. Next in line is central Scotland, where first frosts often arrive between the end of September and the first two weeks of October. The English Midlands, central Ireland and Dublin are next, around the last week of October. They are followed by the rest of inland England and Wales and the coasts of Scotland and western Ireland in the first week or so of November. The east coast of England starts to get frosts around mid- to late November, with the south and west coasts of England and the Gulf Stream-favoured parts of the west coast of Scotland and western Ireland as late as early December. The Scillies and the Channel Islands often get away scot-free. Take this guide with a pinch of driveway salt: first frost dates vary greatly year by year, so use it as a guide to getting ahead, not a chance to procrastinate.

Average temperatures (°C):	Inverness 9, Padstow 11
Average sunshine hours per day:	Inverness 3, Padstow 4
Average days of rainfall:	Inverness 20, Padstow 24
Average rainfall total (mm):	Inverness 30, Padstow 95

Day length

During the course of October, day length decreases by:

2 hours 24 minutes (to 9 hours 8 minutes) – Inverness
1 hour 50 minutes (to 9 hours 49 minutes) – Padstow

Sunrise and set

	Inverness		Padstow	
	Rise	Set	Rise	Set
1st	07.19	18.52	07.19	18.58
2nd	07.22	18.49	07.20	18.56
3rd	07.24	18.46	07.22	18.54
4th	07.26	18.43	07.24	18.52
5th	07.28	18.41	07.25	18.49
6th	07.30	18.38	07.27	18.47
7th	07.32	18.35	07.28	18.45
8th	07.34	18.33	07.30	18.43
9th	07.37	18.30	07.32	18.41
10th	07.39	18.27	07.33	18.39
11th	07.41	18.24	07.35	18.36
12th	07.43	18.22	07.36	18.34
13th	07.45	18.19	07.38	18.32
14th	07.47	18.16	07.40	18.30
15th	07.50	18.14	07.41	18.28
16th	07.52	18.11	07.43	18.26
17th	07.54	18.09	07.44	18.24
18th	07.56	18.06	07.46	18.22
19th	07.58	18.03	07.48	18.20
20th	08.01	18.01	07.49	18.18
21st	08.03	17.58	07.51	18.16
22nd	08.05	17.56	07.53	18.14
23rd	08.07	17.53	07.54	18.12
24th	08.10	17.51	07.56	18.10
25th	08.12	17.48	07.58	18.08
26th	08.14	17.46	07.59	18.06
27th	07.16	16.43	07.01	17.04
28th	07.19	16.41	07.03	17.03
29th	07.21	16.38	07.05	17.01
30th	07.23	16.36	07.06	16.59
31st	07.25	16.34	07.08	16.57

British Summer Time ends on 27th October at 02.00, and this is accounted for above.

O

THE SEA

Average sea temperature

Isle of Lewis:	12.3°C
Whitby:	12.7°C
Belfast:	13.4°C
Cork:	14.2°C
Swansea:	15.2°C
Brighton:	16.3°C
Falmouth:	14.7°C

Spring and neap tides

The spring tides are the most extreme tides of the month, with the highest rises and falls, and the neap tides are the least extreme, with the smallest. Exact timings vary around the coast, but expect them around the following dates:

Spring tides: 14th–15th and 29th–30th

Neap tides: 6th–7th and 22nd–23rd

In the tide timetable opposite, spring tides are shown with an asterisk.

October tide timetable for Dover

For your local high tide differences on Dover, see page 8.

	High water		Low water	
	Morning	Afternoon	Morning	Afternoon
1st	01.13	13.34	08.53	21.16
2nd	01.53	14.16	09.29	21.52
3rd	02.36	14.59	10.04	22.27
4th	03.21	15.46	10.39	23.03
5th	04.12	16.40	11.19	23.47
6th	05.12	17.43	–	12.13
7th	06.21	19.01	00.53	13.34
8th	07.44	20.56	02.16	15.02
9th	09.09	22.01	03.37	16.20
10th	10.04	22.42	04.45	17.18
11th	10.44	23.13	05.36	18.01
12th	11.17	23.38	06.15	18.35
13th	11.48	–	06.47	19.04
14th	00.04	12.16	07.15	19.33 *
15th	00.30	12.42	07.44	20.03 *
16th	00.55	13.06	08.16	20.35
17th	01.19	13.33	08.47	21.05
18th	01.47	14.03	09.19	21.36
19th	02.21	14.40	09.52	22.10
20th	03.03	15.26	10.31	22.53
21th	03.56	16.29	11.20	23.49
22nd	05.24	18.41	–	12.30
23rd	07.23	20.05	01.19	14.14
24th	08.34	21.09	03.03	15.35
25th	09.32	22.03	04.15	16.42
26th	10.21	22.50	05.17	17.43
27th	10.07	22.33	05.13	17.39
28th	10.49	23.12	06.03	18.28
29th	11.31	23.51	06.47	19.12 *
30th	–	12.11	07.27	19.50 *
31st	00.31	12.53	08.03	20.25

British Summer Time ends on 27th October at 02.00, and this is accounted for above.

THE SKY AT NIGHT

Moon phases

1st quarter – 5th October

Full moon – 13th October

3rd quarter – 21st October

New moon – 28th October

In the night sky this month

5th   Close approach of the moon and Saturn, first visible as dusk falls at about 19.00 at an altitude of 16 degrees above the southern horizon. They set at 22.30 in the southwest. Jupiter is also visible until about 20.30.

Moon rise and set

	Inverness		Padstow		
	Rise	Set	Rise	Set	
1st	10.52	20.19	10.35	20.44	
2nd	12.20	20.41	11.54	21.14	
3rd	13.42	21.10	13.09	21.50	
4th	14.55	21.48	14.16	22.34	
5th	15.55	22.37	15.14	23.24	1st quarter
6th	16.41	23.37	16.02	–	
7th	17.15	–	16.41	00.21	
8th	17.39	00.44	17.12	01.23	
9th	17.58	01.55	17.38	02.27	
10th	18.13	03.08	17.59	03.32	
11th	18.26	04.20	18.19	04.37	
12th	18.37	05.33	18.37	05.43	
13th	18.48	06.46	18.55	06.48	full moon
14th	19.00	07.59	19.14	07.54	
15th	19.14	09.14	19.34	09.02	
16th	19.30	10.30	19.58	10.10	
17th	19.52	11.47	20.27	11.20	
18th	20.22	13.03	21.03	12.28	
19th	21.03	14.13	21.49	13.33	
20th	22.00	15.12	22.46	14.31	
21st	23.11	15.58	23.54	15.21	3rd quarter
22nd	–	16.32	–	16.02	
23rd	00.35	16.58	01.09	16.36	
24th	02.04	17.17	02.30	17.04	
25th	03.37	17.34	03.53	17.29	
26th	05.10	17.48	05.17	17.52	
27th	05.43	17.03	05.41	17.15	
28th	07.16	17.20	07.04	17.40	new moon
29th	08.48	17.39	08.27	18.09	
30th	10.16	18.05	09.46	18.43	
31st	11.37	18.39	10.59	19.23	

British Summer Time ends on 27th October at 02.00, and this is accounted for above.

O

Meteor shower of the month – the Draconids

This meteor shower is considered a bit of a 'sleeper', which means even at its peak on the night of the 8th you could be out cricking your neck for a long time and see nothing. But every now and then it produces a surprise impressive display: at its height in October 2011, observers spotted 600 meteors per hour. The trails are particularly languid, taking their time streaking across the sky, and unlike most meteor showers they are best seen in the evening rather than pre-dawn. The Draconids shower is caused by the earth passing through the orbit of Comet 21P/Giacobini-Zinner and its dust and debris burning up on contact with our atmosphere. Comet 21P/Giacobini-Zinner comes close to earth every 6.6 years, and was visited by the International Cometary Explorer spacecraft on its 1985 pass.

NATURE

Inside the beehive in October

Just as all sources of nectar for the bees are drying up, ivy comes to the rescue, coming into copious flower in October. It is covered in bees and wasps seeking out the last of summer's sweetness and sustenance. A hive near ivy may find enough food to spur the queen into laying a final brood of eggs to be raised by the colony; these new young winter bees will live for six months and carry the colony into next spring. The beekeeper will 'heft' the hive around now to see if it contains enough honey to see the hive through winter. The bees will have the honey in the brood box to overwinter on, and the beekeeper may leave one or two 'supers' (boxes of frames) full of honey as well. However, some beekeepers prefer to keep all the bees in a smaller area to help them stay warm through the cold winter nights, and to top up through winter with sugar water should the honey run low.

Look out for...mushrooms

With autumn rains come autumn mushrooms. Mushrooms are the tip of the fungal iceberg: below the ground the fungus will comprise an often vast network of mycelium, strands of fungus that absorb nutrients and moisture from the ground, sustaining it all year round. The fungus exists almost entirely out of sight for most of the year, but autumn rains signal that it is time to fruit and to spread its spores. The mushroom we see is the fruiting body, which will emit microscopic spores that can spread on the wind, alight elsewhere and create new fungal life.

O

NATIVE TREES – SEEDS

OAK

ASH

BEECH

LIME

FIELD MAPLE

THE GARDEN

Planting by the moon

New moon to 1st quarter: 28th September–5th. Sow crops that develop below ground. Dig the soil.

1st quarter to full moon: 5th–13th. Sow crops that develop above ground. Plant seedlings and young plants.

Full moon to 3rd quarter: 13th–21st. Harvest crops for immediate eating. Harvest fruit.

3rd quarter to new moon: 21st–28th. Prune. Harvest for storage. Fertilise and mulch the soil.

Job of the month – plant bulbs

Daffodils must go in early in the autumn, so move quickly. Crocuses, scillas and puschkinias (all of which will be a real boon to early flying bees next spring) should be planted now and are little enough to fit around other plantings, or in containers. Buy tulip bulbs now but plant them in November.

Glut of the month – cooking apples

Apples are ripe on the trees and are lying under them turning cidery. Cooking apples store well, so wrap some in newspaper for the shed and for winter.

- **Eve's pudding:** Pour a layer of Bramley purée into a baking dish and top with a sponge mixture: 150g butter creamed with 150g caster sugar, 3 eggs beaten in, and 150g self-raising flour folded in. Bake at 190°c, Gas Mark 5 for about 30 minutes or until the top is firm. Serve hot with custard or double cream.
- **Buttered apples:** Bramleys turn to fluff, but this will work with most others. Peel, core and slice the apples into wedges, then fry in butter until brown. Add sugar and cinnamon, and cook for a few minutes. Remove the slices from the pan and tip a glass of cider into the pan. Simmer, stirring, then stir in double cream and a little butter. Pour over the apples and serve.

O

Flower of the month – marigold

Latin name: *Calendula officinalis* (*Calendula* from the Latin *kalendae*, meaning 'calendar' or 'first day of the month', either from the plant's efficacy in treating menstrual disorders or from the fact that they bloom most months of the year; *officinalis* indicates medicinal properties and uses).
Common names: pot marigold, ruddles, Scotch marigold, marybud, holligold.

The name marigold comes from Mary's gold, as they are in vibrant flower during the Feast of the Annunciation of Mary on 25th March. Clearly, March is at the other end of the year, but as the Latin name *Calendula* points out, marigolds flower all year round, and they are certainly blooming now in their Hallowe'en-friendly shades of pumpkin and fallen leaf. Another plant that goes by the name is the Aztec marigold, *Tagetes erecta*, which is strongly associated with the Mexican Day of the Dead, *Día de Muertos* (which itself has connections to Hallowe'en). They are used as glowing orange grave decorations, to attract the souls of the dead. Calendulas themselves have links to witchcraft, weather divining and medicine. Hung over a doorway, they ward off evil, and if a marigold hasn't opened by 07.00, there will be a thunderstorm. Marigolds' medicinal uses are many: to treat stomach ulcers, menstrual cramps, dermatitis, skin inflammations, burns and more. They are edible, too – sprinkle some petals over your Hallowe'en pumpkin soup.

These annuals should be sown in spring, or in autumn for early flowers next year. They are great self-seeders, so once might be enough.

THE KITCHEN

Cheese of the month – Berkswell

This beautiful and complex hard ewes' cheese started life as
an experiment in producing Caerphilly by cheese makers Ram
Hall Farm in Warwickshire, but it soon developed down its own
path. Matured for four to six months until it is hard and nutty,
it is closest in style to a Pecorino or Manchego cheese and, like
Manchego, is wonderful paired with membrillo or another
fruit cheese. Ram Hall has its own flock of milking sheep
and manages it so that the cheese can be made year round.
However, the milk is unpasteurised, which allows its changing
flavours to come through strongly in the cheese. The fruity and
tangy notes are stronger in summer, with the more caramel,
nutty and toasted notes to the fore in autumn. Younger cheeses
are generally sweeter and creamier with stronger, more intense
flavours, while a drier, more crumbly texture develops as the
cheese matures. It's wonderful in cooking in place of Parmesan
or even Cheddar.

In season

This is wild mushroom season. Look for **ceps, chanterelles** and
puffballs in specialist delis. **White truffles** are in season.

The season for greenhouse vegetables is coming to a close.
Though there are still **aubergines, tomatoes** and **chillies** to
be had, the temperature will dictate how long they keep on
producing. The more unusual autumn root vegetables are now
ready to harvest: **salsify, scorzonera** and **Jerusalem artichokes**,
and there are plenty of **beetroot, carrots** and **parsnips** around.
Kale and **cabbage** are ready to eat on the veg plot.

Tree fruit – **apples, pears, quinces, medlars** – is at its best in
October. **Grapes** are maturing and you can still find the last **figs**
and **blackberries**.

Hunting season is fully under way now, and you may find
duck, goose, grouse, guinea fowl, hare, pheasant, rabbit and
venison in specialist butchers.

This is the end of the **mackerel** season. There is plenty
of **hake, lemon sole** and **sardines. Oysters** are back in season.

O

RECIPES

Poached and roasted quince with cheese

Quince only yields its delicious flavour after long cooking. If you have a glut you might want to make membrillo, the fruit cheese (super-thick quince jam) traditionally eaten with Manchego cheese. But you can make a souped-down version by poaching and then baking one or two. These can be eaten hot with cream or ice cream, or left to cool and served with cheese. Cooking time is slightly up to you: the longer you cook them, the deeper the ruby colour they will take on, but the soft coral afforded impatient cooks is beautiful, too.

Serves 4, as part of a cheeseboard
Ingredients
600ml water
300ml apple juice
Juice of 1 lemon
250g sugar
1 star anise
1 bay leaf
2 quince

Method
Make up the poaching liquid first, putting all of the ingredients, apart from the quince, into a saucepan, and heating gently to dissolve the sugar. Peel, quarter and core the quince and put them into the liquid, then simmer gently for about an hour.

Preheat the oven to 190°c, Gas Mark 5 and transfer the quinces to a roasting dish with a little of their juice. Bake for at least 30 minutes, or until they reach the shade you want them. Leave them to cool and then serve with a hard cheese such as Berkswell or Manchego.

Pot-roast pheasant with apples, cider, porcini and chestnuts

Pheasant is the most plentiful and widely available game bird in the UK, and its season begins on 1st October. It is also a good choice if you are new to game, as its flavour is subtler and less gamey than most other game birds. The flesh can be dry, but pot-roasting and slow cooking make it deliciously tender.

Serves 4
Ingredients
15g dried porcini
50g butter
2 pheasants, tied
1 tablespoon plain flour, seasoned with salt and pepper
2 rashers of smoked streaky bacon
A few juniper berries, crushed
10 shallots, peeled and trimmed
100g cooked and peeled chestnuts
150g dried Puy or green lentils, washed
500ml cider
300ml chicken stock
2 eating apples, each cored and cut into 6 pieces
Small bunch of thyme
1 bay leaf
150ml double cream
salt and pepper

O

Method
Preheat the oven to 180°C, Gas Mark 4. Soak the dried porcini in 100ml water for 10 minutes, then drain them, reserving the mushroom water.

Melt the butter in a large casserole on the hob. Dust the pheasants with the seasoned flour and put them into the casserole, frying them for a couple of minutes on each side and then turning, until they are browned on all sides. Remove them from the casserole and set aside.

Cut the bacon into strips and fry it in the casserole (adding a little more butter if needed), along with the juniper berries, the shallots and then the chestnuts. When the bacon is crisp, add the lentils and stir them in the flavoured butter. Pour on the cider and bring to the boil, using it to deglaze the casserole and making sure there is no flour residue left that will burn during the cooking. Add the chicken stock, the mushrooms and mushroom water, apple slices and herbs, and bring to the boil. Put the pheasants back into the casserole, along with any resting juices, seal tightly with a lid or with foil and place in the oven. Bake for about 1 hour 45 minutes.

Remove the casserole from the oven, and put the birds on a warmed plate under foil and tea towels to keep warm. Place the casserole on the hob over a medium heat, and add the cream to the sauce, and then salt and pepper to taste. Tip the lentils and sauce on to a platter and put the birds on top; serve immediately.

Soul cakes

These are old English traditional cakes. On All Hallows' Eve, All Saints' Day and All Souls' Day, children went 'souling', singing for soul cakes from house to house – very likely a precursor to trick-or-treating. (See page 220 for the song they sang).

Makes 12–15 cakes
Ingredients
175g butter
175g caster sugar
3 egg yolks
450g self-raising flour, plus extra for dusting
2 teaspoons mixed spice
A few gratings of nutmeg
About 100ml milk
100g currants, plus a handful more to decorate

Method

Preheat the oven to 190°C, Gas Mark 5. Cream the butter with the sugar until it is light and fluffy and then beat in the egg yolks, one at a time. In a separate bowl sieve the flour and the spices together and add to the butter mixture along with the currants (reserving those for decoration). Mix all together with a wooden spoon and then add the milk and go in with your hands to pull everything together into a dough.

On a lightly floured surface, roll out the dough to a thickness of around 1cm, and cut out rounds with a biscuit cutter. Make a slight cross indent in the top of each with a palette knife, and then push currants along it. Place the rounds on baking parchment on a baking tray, and bake for 10–15 minutes or until golden. Allow to cool on a rack before eating.

O

A SONG FOR HALLOWE'EN

'Soul Cake'
Traditional

From medieval times right up to the 1930s, children went a-souling door to door on Hallowe'en. This was the song they sang in the hope of winning a soul cake or two from their neighbours. For a recipe for Soul Cake, see page 219.

A soul, a soul, a soul - cake, Please, good miss - us a

soul - cake, An ap ple, a pear, a plum or a cher - ry,

An - y good thing to make us all mer - ry. One for Pet - er,

two for Paul, Three for Him that made us all.

God bless the master of this house and the mistress also
And all the little children that around your table grow,
Likewise your men and maidens, your cattle and your store
And all that dwells within your gates,
We wish you ten times more.

> *Chorus:*
> *A soul, a soul, a soul cake,*
> *Please, good missus, a soul cake,*
> *An apple, a pear, a plum or a cherry,*
> *Any good thing to make us all merry.*
> *One for Peter, two for Paul,*
> *Three for Him that made us all.*

The lanes are very dirty and my shoes are very thin,
I've got a little pocket I can put a penny in.
If you haven't got a penny, a ha'penny will do,
If you haven't got a ha'penny, then God bless you.

O

November

- **1** Samhain (Pagan)
- **1** All Saints' Day (Christian)
- **2** All Souls' Day (Christian)
- **2** Bridgwater Carnival, Somerset
- **5** Guy Fawkes Night
- **10** Prophet's birthday (Muslim)
- **10** Remembrance Sunday
- **11** Remembrance Day/Armistice Day
- **11** Martinmas
- **24** Stir-up Sunday – make your Christmas pudding
- **30** St Andrew's Day – patron saint of Scotland

The naming of November

> Samhain (Scots Gaelic)
> November (Scots/Ulster Scots)
> Samhain (Irish Gaelic)
> Mee Houney (Manx)
> Tachwed (Welsh)
> Du (Cornish)
> Novembre (Jèrriais)

The pre-Christian Celtic year began on 1st November, with the festival of Samhain, one of the four markers of the Celtic year (the others being Imbolc, Beltane and Lughnasadh). Samhain marks the beginning of winter and was the time the cattle were brought in from the pastures to their winter quarters. The word may be derived from the Proto-Indo-European *sam*, meaning 'together'. Samhain was considered a time when the spirits of the dead could return to the earth, with the veil between the living and the dead especially thin. The word for November in Scots Gaelic and Irish Gaelic is Samhain, while the Manx name, Mee Houney, is derived from it.

The Welsh Tachwed takes a different direction and means 'slaughter' (much as the Anglo-Saxon word for November was *Blotmonath*, meaning 'blood month'). This is because November was the traditional time to slaughter and preserve the meat of farm animals, fattened up over summer. The Cornish name, Du, again leans towards the Breton name for the month (also *Du*) and means 'black', perhaps related to the shortening days.

A CHRISTIAN TALE FOR NOVEMBER

All Saints, All Souls and remembrance

In 3rd-century Rome, Christians were not welcome. The Roman people found converts to this almost new religion threatening and unsettling. Why wouldn't they make animal sacrifices like everybody else? Why did they worship secretly in their own homes? And worst of all, why was their loyalty to their God and not to the Roman state? They were seen as corrosive to society and were blamed for natural disasters: if you do not worship the pantheon of Roman gods correctly, what do you expect to happen?

Persecution was common but piecemeal and often mob-led, and the death of each Christian martyr was marked by the Christian community annually. And then along came Decius, Roman emperor from 249 to 251. He issued a decree requiring Christians to carry out a public act of sacrifice as a testimony of allegiance to the empire. Refusal was punished by imprisonment, torture and execution.

Yet many refused, and the number of martyrs grew so great that it became impossible to mark the date of each martyrdom. The Christian Church adopted a common day for all: the Feast of All Saints, or All Saints' Day. This was at first celebrated annually on 13th May but later was moved to 1st November by Pope Gregory III in the 8th century. It then coincided – deliberately perhaps – with the Celtic pagan celebration of Samhain, which is itself a commemoration of the dead, of lost relatives and friends, and is considered a time when the veil between the worlds of the living and the dead is at its thinnest.

In the 11th century, 2nd November was chosen as All Souls' Day, a day to remember all of the faithful who have died. And later still, early November became the time to remember another mass loss of life – in World War I – on Remembrance Day and Remembrance Sunday. It seems that these quiet, dark moments in the year lend themselves to contemplation, appreciation and commemoration of lost loved ones.

N

WEATHER

Mellow mists

With the lengthening of nights come mists and fogs. Overnight, the ground can now become cool enough that when it meets moisture-filled air it chills it to dew point – changing the moisture held in it from invisible water vapour to visible droplets. Air movement in the form of gentle winds keeps these tiny droplets afloat, and a mist or a fog is formed. Both are burned off from the ground upwards: the sun's rays must first penetrate through the fog and warm the ground, which in turn raises the temperature of the air layer above it, and that turns the droplets back into invisible water vapour.

Average temperatures (°C):	Inverness 6, Padstow 8
Average sunshine hours per day:	Inverness 2, Padstow 3
Average days of rainfall:	Inverness 19, Padstow 24
Average rainfall total (mm):	Inverness 20, Padstow 110

Day length

During the course of November, day length decreases by:

1 hour 54 minutes (to 7 hours 9 minutes) – Inverness
1 hour 23 minutes (to 8 hours 22 minutes) – Padstow

Sunrise and set

	Inverness		Padstow	
	Rise	Set	Rise	Set
1st	07.28	16.31	07.10	16.55
2nd	07.30	16.29	07.11	16.54
3rd	07.32	16.27	07.13	16.52
4th	07.35	16.25	07.15	16.50
5th	07.37	16.22	07.16	16.49
6th	07.39	16.20	07.18	16.47
7th	07.41	16.18	07.20	16.45
8th	07.44	16.16	07.22	16.44
9th	07.46	16.14	07.23	16.42
10th	07.48	16.12	07.25	16.41
11th	07.50	16.10	07.27	16.39
12th	07.53	16.08	07.28	16.38
13th	07.55	16.06	07.30	16.36
14th	07.57	16.04	07.32	16.35
15th	07.59	16.02	07.33	16.34
16th	08.02	16.00	07.35	16.32
17th	08.04	15.58	07.37	16.31
18th	08.06	15.56	07.38	16.30
19th	08.08	15.55	07.40	16.29
20th	08.10	15.53	07.41	16.28
21st	08.12	15.51	07.43	16.27
22nd	08.14	15.50	07.45	16.26
23rd	08.16	15.48	07.46	16.25
24th	08.19	15.47	07.48	16.24
25th	08.21	15.45	07.49	16.23
26th	08.23	15.44	07.51	16.22
27th	08.24	15.43	07.52	16.21
28th	08.26	15.42	07.54	16.20
29th	08.28	15.40	07.55	16.20
30th	08.30	15.39	07.56	16.19

N

THE SEA

Average sea temperature

Isle of Lewis:	11.2°C
Whitby:	10.7°C
Belfast:	12.3°C
Cork:	12.7°C
Swansea:	13.5°C
Brighton:	14.7°C
Falmouth:	13.3°C

Spring and neap tides

The spring tides are the most extreme tides of the month, with the highest rises and falls, and the neap tides are the least extreme, with the smallest. Exact timings vary around the coast, but expect them around the following dates:

Spring tides: 13th–14th and 27th–28th

Neap tides: 5th–6th and 20th–21st

In the tide timetable opposite, spring tides are shown with an asterisk.

November tide timetable for Dover

For your local high tide differences on Dover, see page 8.

	High water		Low water	
	Morning	Afternoon	Morning	Afternoon
1st	01.13	13.35	08.39	20.59
2nd	01.57	14.21	09.14	21.32
3rd	02.46	15.14	09.50	22.09
4th	03.42	16.14	10.38	23.04
5th	04.46	17.24	11.54	–
6th	05.57	18.51	00.33	13.20
7th	07.16	20.12	01.53	14.31
8th	08.18	20.58	02.58	15.28
9th	09.02	21.30	03.50	16.13
10th	09.38	21.59	04.32	16.51
11th	10.09	22.28	05.08	17.26
12th	10.39	22.57	05.43	18.02
13th	11.08	23.26	06.17	18.37 *
14th	11.38	23.56	06.52	19.12 *
15th	–	12.10	07.27	19.45
16th	00.29	12.47	08.02	20.19
17th	01.09	13.28	08.39	20.56
18th	01.55	14.19	09.21	21.42
19th	02.54	15.29	10.13	22.39
20th	04.17	17.17	11.23	–
21st	05.50	18.40	00.02	12.51
22nd	07.04	19.45	01.32	14.07
23rd	08.05	20.40	02.43	15.14
24th	08.57	21.29	03.47	16.17
25th	09.45	22.13	04.45	17.14
26th	10.29	22.54	05.37	18.04
27th	11.12	23.34	06.22	18.48 *
28th	11.53	–	07.04	19.27 *
29th	00.14	12.35	07.42	20.02
30th	00.55	13.16	08.19	20.35

N

THE SKY AT NIGHT

Moon phases

1st quarter – 4th November

Full moon – 12th November

3rd quarter – 19th November

New moon – 26th November

In the night sky this month

2nd   Close approach of the moon and Saturn, first visible as dusk falls at about 17.00 at an altitude of 15 degrees above the southern horizon. They set around 20.00 in the west.

Moon rise and set

	Inverness		Padstow		
	Rise	Set	Rise	Set	
1st	12.46	19.24	12.04	20.12	
2nd	13.39	20.22	12.58	21.08	
3rd	14.18	21.28	13.41	22.10	
4th	14.46	22.39	14.15	23.14	1st quarter
5th	15.06	23.52	14.43	–	
6th	15.22	–	15.06	00.20	
7th	15.35	01.05	15.25	01.25	
8th	15.46	02.18	15.44	02.31	
9th	15.57	03.31	16.01	03.36	
10th	16.08	04.44	16.19	04.42	
11th	16.21	05.59	16.39	05.50	
12th	16.36	07.16	17.02	06.59	full moon
13th	16.56	08.35	17.29	08.09	
14th	17.22	09.53	18.03	09.20	
15th	18.00	11.06	18.46	10.27	
16th	18.52	12.10	19.39	11.29	
17th	19.59	13.01	20.43	12.21	
18th	21.18	13.38	21.56	13.05	
19th	22.45	14.05	23.14	13.39	3rd quarter
20th	–	14.25	–	14.08	
21st	00.14	14.41	00.34	14.33	
22nd	01.44	14.56	01.54	14.55	
23rd	03.14	15.09	03.15	15.17	
24th	04.44	15.24	04.37	15.40	
25th	06.15	15.41	05.58	16.06	
26th	07.45	16.03	07.19	16.37	new moon
27th	09.11	16.32	08.36	17.13	
28th	10.27	17.11	09.46	17.59	
29th	11.29	18.04	10.47	18.52	
30th	12.16	19.08	11.36	19.53	

N

Meteor shower of the month – the Leonids

The Leonids are famed for their occasional and extremely intense meteor storms, which turn them from their usual 15-meteors-per-hour appearance into a thrilling spectacle of thousands of trails per minute. The 1833 shower was particularly intense, with an estimate of 100,000 meteors per hour, and the storms of 1999, 2001 and 2002 boasted around 3,000 per hour. These peaks have sometimes occurred because the parent Comet 55P/Tempel-Tuttle's orbit intersected almost exactly with earth's, meaning that we hit the centre of the trail rather than the spread-out debris, and sometimes because of the comet having recently made a new circuit of its 33-year orbit. Comet 55P/Tempel-Tuttle had a close brush with Jupiter not long ago, which is thought likely to have shifted its path and that of its debris streams, making such astonishing displays unlikely in the near future at least. It peaks this year on the night of the 17th and early morning of the 18th.

THE KITCHEN

Cheese of the month – Sparkenhoe Vintage Red Leicester

Artisan-made Red Leicester is a different beast from the stuff in square supermarket packets, mainly because of the starter culture used. 'Helveticus' is the starter culture of choice for the mass-produced cheeses (Cheddar, too), quickly producing bland, fairly sweet, consistent cheese. By contrast, Leicestershire Handmade Cheese Company uses a mixture of slow-working bacteria to make Sparkenhoe Red Leicester, allowing the flavours of the raw, unpasteurised milk to come through, and making each batch individual. Normal Sparkenhoe is matured for six months and 'vintage' for eighteen months, so the November batches were made with spring milk from cows that had been out in the field for a month or two. During the extra 12 months' maturation, the flavour strengthens, small protein crystals appear throughout and the red annatto colouring deepens. (This natural plant dye, incidentally, was first added as a marketing gimmick to make the cheese stand out from the creamy-coloured rest.)

In season

From the vegetable patch, there are **Jerusalem artichokes, carrots, beetroot, leeks, parsnips, cauliflower, Brussels sprouts, kale** and **winter cabbage**, along with stored **maincrop potatoes, borlotti beans** and **winter squash**.

Cranberries, satsumas, clementines and **pomegranates** are starting to arrive. There are plenty of **apples, pears** and **quince**.

Nuts are plentiful: **hazelnuts, sweet chestnuts** and **walnuts** have all recently ripened.

Lots of **wild mushrooms** are still around and **white truffles** are in season.

Duck, goose, grouse, guinea fowl, partridge, pheasant, venison and **wood pigeon** are all in season.

Brill, sardine, skate, clams, mussels and **oysters** are plentiful.

N

RECIPES

Martinmas beef

The Feast of St Martin – Martinmas – on 11th November was once an important date in the agricultural year. The annual wheat seeding was completed by this day, and hiring fairs were held to engage the following year's workforce. St Martin is the patron saint of wine growers, and this was the first day that you could taste your new wine. It was also traditionally the day for the annual slaughter of cattle, most of their meat being spiced, salted and stored for the winter. As Martin is also the patron saint of beggars, an ox was traditionally slaughtered to be given to the poor. Thus, it was a day for universal feasting, often on something beefy and spicy.

Serves 6
Ingredients
1300g rolled brisket
2 tablespoons sunflower oil
2 large onions, thinly sliced
5 garlic cloves
2 bay leaves
2.5cm fresh root ginger, peeled and grated
½ teaspoon ground cloves
½ teaspoon ground mace
1 bottle of red wine
10 small carrots, peeled
Salt and pepper

Method
Preheat the oven to 180°C, Gas Mark 4. Season the brisket all over with salt and pepper and then heat the oil in a large

casserole and brown the meat all over. Transfer it to a plate, discarding any excess fat. Put all of the ingredients, except for the wine and carrots, in the casserole and lay the brisket on top, then pour on the wine. Heat on the hob until bubbling. Cover, transfer to the oven and cook for 3 hours. Nestle in the carrots and cook for a further 30–60 minutes with the lid off, until the meat is tender and the sauce is thickened. Serve accompanied by dauphinoise or mashed potatoes.

Bonfire toffee apples

Bonfire toffee is the dark toffee rich in black treacle, associated with Bonfire Night and particularly loved in the north of England. It is so hard that it has to be smashed into pieces when made in a tray, but is slightly easier to eat wrapped around apples on sticks. Only partake if you are confident of your fillings! Any eating apples will work, but those with a sharp or very distinctive flavour will be particularly good. You will need a sugar thermometer.

Makes 8 toffee apples

Ingredients

8 apples

8 sticks (apple tree prunings look great)

Sunflower oil

125ml hot water

450g muscovado sugar

115g black treacle

115g golden syrup

¼ teaspoon cream of tartar

N

Method

Put the apples into a large bowl, pour a kettle of boiled water over them, and leave for a few minutes to remove the waxy coating that would prevent the toffee from sticking. Pour away the water and pat the apples dry, then remove their stalks and push a stick into each. Put parchment paper on a flat baking tray, and rub it all over with oil. Line a small baking tray with baking parchment, and oil that well, too, ready for any excess toffee.

Gently heat the water and the sugar in a heavy-bottomed saucepan, without stirring (you can swish the pan a little if you need to) until the sugar has dissolved. Oil a bowl and measure the black treacle and the golden syrup into it, then pour that into the sugar and water mixture. Add the cream of tartar, and swish again to lightly mix everything. Turn up the heat and bring the mixture to the boil. Continue boiling until it reaches 140°C on the sugar thermometer, sometimes labelled 'soft crack' (this may take some time but don't leave the toffee unattended).

As soon as it reaches that point, remove it from the heat and work quickly to roll your apples in the toffee, letting the excess drip off (you want as thin a coating as possible) and then placing them 'stick up' on the oiled parchment. Pour any excess onto the lined small baking tray. Leave to cool completely. The toffee in the small baking tray will have to be smashed into shards with a hammer, in the traditional manner.

THE GARDEN

Planting by the moon

New moon to 1st quarter: 28th October–4th. Sow crops that develop below ground. Dig the soil.

1st quarter to full moon: 4th–12th. Sow crops that develop above ground. Plant seedlings and young plants.

Full moon to 3rd quarter: 12th–19th. Harvest crops for immediate eating. Harvest fruit.

3rd quarter to new moon: 19th–26th. Prune. Harvest for storage. Fertilise and mulch the soil.

Job of the month – plant roses

If you made a list of roses back in June, order and plant them now. You can buy them as bare-root plants, which establish much better than pot-grown plants, as well as being cheaper and available in more variety. 'Gertrude Jekyll', 'Madame Alfred Carrière', 'De Rêscht' and 'Louise Odier' have beautiful blooms and particularly good scents, if you are undecided.

Glut of the month – Jerusalem artichoke

Jerusalem artichokes taste deliciously nutty, but are unpopular because of their windy side effects. An occasional treat, maybe.

- **Hasselbacked Jerusalem artichokes:** Peel the tubers then make a series of parallel slices mostly, but not fully, through each. Roll in oil and salt, and then roast at 190°C, Gas Mark 5 until crispy.
- **Jerusalem artichoke soup:** Steam the tubers first. Fry an onion, some garlic and some bacon pieces, then combine all with chicken or vegetable stock and milk, and blend together. Heat through, season and eat.
- **Jerusalem artichoke boulangère:** Thinly slice peeled artichokes (drop them into lemon water or they discolour) then layer in a dish with sautéed onions. Pour in stock to halfway up the dish, cover tightly and bake at 180°C, Gas Mark 4 for 1½ hours.

N

Flower of the month – chrysanthemum

Latin name: *Chrysanthemum* (from Ancient Greek *chrysos*, meaning 'golden' and *anthos*, meaning flower)
Common names: chrysanth, xanth, mums, pot mums.

Just when every other flower in the cutting garden is packing up for autumn and winter, chrysanthemums start to bloom. And they do so in a riot of colours and shapes: some huge, single, with voluptuous incurved or spidery-thin petals, others sweet and mumsy with a spray of smiley pastel daisy flowers; some dramatic velvet red and rich orange, others zingy greens and acid yellows. The vast variety is a testament to enthusiastic and imaginative cultivation and breeding by Japanese gardeners, from the early 8th century onwards.

The chrysanthemum has become closely tied to the French celebration of All Saints' Day, known there as *La Toussaint*. On 1st November, French families gather to visit and tend to the graves of their loved ones and brighten them up with pots of chrysanthemums. Every graveyard is a riot of colour by the end of the day. This connection may be due to the chrysanthemum starting to flower in the darkest times, and its ability to regenerate in spring. The chrysanthemum was originally chosen to be the flower of Remembrance Sunday, before the poppy became the official flower in 1921, and chrysanthemums are still laid on French war graves on All Souls' Day, 2nd November.

CHRYSANTHEMUM TYPES

NATURE

Inside the beehive in November

All bee activity is starting to close down as the nights lengthen and the weather cools, and the bees rarely leave the hive. They must fill their stomachs with honey from their stored supplies in order to keep their body temperature up, and any foray outside will require more fuel. It is better to sit tight. Bees will naturally die through the winter, and as colonies get smaller they can be at great risk from harsh conditions. But strong colonies containing plenty of bees and a young queen can withstand a very harsh winter. They may even raise a small brood when the weather is mild, though mostly the queen will take a rest now and conserve her own energy. The beekeeper will fit a mouse excluder over the entrance – a piece of metal with bee-sized holes – as mice like to enter beehives in winter and nest there for the ready supply of food.

Look out for...rookeries

As leaves fall from trees, rookeries become easier to spot. Rooks make bulky, twiggy nests high up in trees and have a habit of gathering together, often in built-up areas. They also make a lot of noise, their cry a harsh and raucous 'kaah!'. All of this combined with their Gothic looks makes people find their presence disturbing, but they are actually highly intelligent and sociable birds.

A SONG FOR REMEMBRANCE

'Far, Far from Wipers'

Most of the songs of World War I came out of music halls, and their purpose was to keep spirits up and morale high among those waiting back at home. The soldiers in the trenches sang their own songs, most often new words set to well-known tunes and hymns, and again they generally had a jaunty air, albeit with a little bit of very British comedy grumbling. Very few gave any hint of the actual horrors endured, and with good reason: their purpose was to help the men keep on, not to encourage them to sink into despair. 'Far, Far from Wipers' is one of the few with a plaintive air and a good dose of reality, short as it is. 'Wipers' was what the British soldiers called the northern French town of Ypres (actually pronounced 'Eep') which was where some of the worst fighting of the war took place.

Far, far from Wi - pers I long to be,

Where Ger - man sni - pers can't get at me.

Damp is my dug out, cold are my feet,

wait - ing for whizz bangs to send me to sleep.

N

December

- **1** Start of meteorological winter
- **1** First Sunday of Advent
- **22** Winter solstice, start of astronomical winter
- **23** First day of Hanukkah (Jewish)
- **24** Christmas Eve (Christian)
- **25** Christmas Day, (Christian) holiday
- **26** Boxing Day/St Stephen's Day, holiday
- **30** Last day of Hanukkah (Jewish)
- **31** New Year's Eve

The naming of December

> Dùbhlachd (Scots Gaelic)
> December (Scots/Ulster Scots)
> Nollaig (Irish Gaelic)
> Mee ny Nollick (Manx)
> Rhagfyr (Welsh)
> Kevardhu (Cornish)
> Dézembre (Jèrriais)

Nollaig (Irish Gaelic) and Mee ny Nollick (Manx) both come from *natalicius*, Latin for 'birthday' or 'birth'. Relating to Christmas, this is the only place where Christianity has left its mark on the names of the month in the languages of the British Isles, and it suggests that these particular names are not as ancient as some. The Welsh Ragfyr means 'foreshortening' and is thought to relate to the shortening of days. In a similar vein, the Scots Gaelic Dùbhlachd, meaning 'black', is concerned with the increasing gloom. Cornish goes one step further, having used up 'black' on November; its name for December is Kevardhu (which is most similar to the Breton name for the month, *Kerzu*) and means 'very black'.

A POLISH CHRISTMAS STORY FOR DECEMBER

Wigilia and the animals

On Christmas Eve at the stroke of midnight, something magical happens in barns, hutches and dog baskets. For one hour only, it is said that animals are given the power of human speech, although only those who have led a blameless life can hear them. This ability is bestowed upon them because of the part they played in the stable in Bethlehem, watching over Jesus in the manger. The ox and the donkey are the only ones that get a Bible mention, and they bowed down to him. But the shepherds must have brought their sheep, and what stable doesn't have a few mice running around in the straw, or a pair of doves in the rafters, or maybe even a small colony of overwintering bees in the cracks between the stones? Christmas lore around the British Isles has it that bees wake from their winter slumber to hum Psalm 100, 'Make a Joyful Noise Unto the Lord'. But such festive animal tales are most widespread in continental Europe, and they have been fully interwoven into Polish Christmas traditions.

Polish families celebrate on Christmas Eve, known as *Wigilia*, meaning 'vigil'. The meal can only begin when the first star of the evening is spotted in the sky, and it always begins with the breaking and sharing of *oplatek*, a thin wafer, pieces of which are also given to each pet or farm animal. The meal comprises 12 courses, one for each of the disciples, and is meat-free, partly in recognition of the animals. Straw is placed under the table or under the tablecloth to remind people of the stable.

Poles have long made up the UK's largest foreign-born and second-generation population, partly because Polish military units based themselves in Britain during Nazi occupation of Poland, and were encouraged to stay after the war in recognition of their war contribution. A great many households around Britain will be looking out for the first star this Christmas Eve.

D

WEATHER

Types of frost
Hoar frost: From 'hoary', meaning 'aged and whitened', in reference to the shaggy and feathery coating that hoar frost leaves. It occurs under calm, cloudless skies, when there is no (or very little) wind, and under 'inversion' conditions: when cold air is trapped under warmer air.

Advection frost: Strong, cold winds prettily rim the edges of objects and plants with tiny spikes of frost, usually pointing in the direction of the wind.

Window frost: Also known poetically as fern frost or ice flowers, this is the frost that creeps across window frames forming swirls, feathers and other patterns, caused by the difference between the very cold air on the outside of the glass and the warmer, moderately moist air on the inside. The growth of the patterns responds to imperfections on the glass surface.

Average temperatures (°C):	Inverness 5, Padstow 6
Average sunshine hours per day:	Inverness 2, Padstow 2
Average days of rainfall:	Inverness 17, Padstow 24
Average rainfall total (mm):	Inverness 40, Padstow 112

Day length
During the course of December, day length:

Decreases by 31 minutes (to minimum 6 hours 35 minutes on 22nd), then increases by 7 minutes by the end of the month – Inverness

Decreases by 21 minutes (to minimum 7 hours 59 minutes on 22nd), then increases by 4 minutes by the end of the month – Padstow

Sunrise and set

	Inverness		*Padstow*	
	Rise	Set	Rise	Set
1st	08.32	15.38	07.58	16.18
2nd	08.34	15.37	07.59	16.18
3rd	08.35	15.36	08.00	16.17
4th	08.37	15.35	08.02	16.17
5th	08.39	15.35	08.03	16.16
6th	08.40	15.34	08.04	16.16
7th	08.42	15.33	08.05	16.16
8th	08.43	15.33	08.06	16.15
9th	08.45	15.32	08.08	16.15
10th	08.46	15.32	08.09	16.15
11th	08.47	15.31	08.10	16.15
12th	08.49	15.31	08.11	16.15
13th	08.50	15.31	08.12	16.15
14th	08.51	15.31	08.13	16.15
15th	08.52	15.31	08.13	16.15
16th	08.53	15.31	08.14	16.15
17th	08.54	15.31	08.15	16.15
18th	08.54	15.31	08.16	16.16
19th	08.55	15.31	08.16	16.16
20th	08.56	15.32	08.17	16.16
21st	08.56	15.32	08.17	16.17
22nd	08.57	15.33	08.18	16.17
23rd	08.57	15.33	08.18	16.18
24th	08.58	15.34	08.19	16.18
25th	08.58	15.35	08.19	16.19
26th	08.58	15.35	08.20	16.20
27th	08.58	15.36	08.20	16.21
28th	08.59	15.37	08.20	16.21
29th	08.59	15.38	08.20	16.22
30th	08.58	15.39	08.20	16.23
31st	08.58	15.40	08.20	16.24

THE SEA

Average sea temperature

Isle of Lewis:	9.8°C
Whitby:	8.9°C
Belfast:	10.5°C
Cork:	11.1°C
Swansea:	11.1°C
Brighton:	11.9°C
Falmouth:	11.8°C

Spring and neap tides

The spring tides are the most extreme tides of the month, with the highest rises and falls, and the neap tides are the least extreme, with the smallest. Exact timings vary around the coast, but expect them around the following dates:

Spring tides: 14th–15th and 27th–28th

Neap tides: 5th–6th and 20th–21st

In the tide timetable opposite, spring tides are shown with an asterisk.

December tide timetable for Dover

For your local high tide differences on Dover, see page 8.

	High water		*Low water*	
	Morning	Afternoon	Morning	Afternoon
1st	01.37	14.00	08.54	21.06
2nd	02.22	14.48	09.28	21.38
3rd	03.11	15.42	10.08	22.20
4th	04.06	16.44	11.02	23.20
5th	05.08	17.51	–	12.15
6th	06.15	19.00	00.44	13.27
7th	07.19	19.56	01.55	14.26
8th	08.10	20.40	02.54	15.19
9th	08.51	21.18	03.44	16.06
10th	09.28	21.53	04.30	16.51
11th	10.05	22.28	05.12	17.33
12th	10.41	23.04	05.53	18.14
13th	11.19	23.41	06.33	18.54
14th	11.57	–	07.13	19.33 *
15th	00.21	12.40	07.53	20.12 *
16th	01.06	13.26	08.36	20.53
17th	01.55	14.19	09.22	21.40
18th	02.52	15.23	10.14	22.35
19th	03.57	16.40	11.15	23.41
20th	05.10	18.03	–	12.24
21st	06.25	19.13	00.54	13.33
22nd	07.33	20.14	02.04	14.39
23rd	08.33	21.07	03.11	15.46
24th	09.26	21.56	04.16	16.50
25th	10.15	22.40	05.14	17.43
26th	11.00	23.21	06.03	18.29
27th	11.41	–	06.47	19.09 *
28th	00.01	12.21	07.27	19.45 *
29th	00.41	13.01	08.04	20.17
30th	01.20	13.40	08.38	20.46
31st	01.59	14.20	09.09	21.14

THE SKY AT NIGHT

Moon phases

1st quarter – 4th December

Full moon – 12th December

3rd quarter – 19th December

New moon – 26th December

In the night sky this month

13th, 14th   Geminids meteor shower.

23rd   Close approach of Mars and the moon, which rise at about 05.00 in the southeast and reach an altitude of 17 degrees above the horizon before becoming lost in the dawn at about 07.30 in the south/southeast.

28th   Close approach of Venus and the moon, which become visible in the dusk 13 degrees above the southwestern horizon at 16.30. They set at around 18.00.

Moon rise and set

	Inverness		Padstow		
	Rise	Set	Rise	Set	
1st	12.49	20.19	12.15	20.58	
2nd	13.12	21.33	12.45	22.04	
3rd	13.30	22.47	13.10	23.10	
4th	13.44	–	13.31	–	1st quarter
5th	13.55	00.00	13.50	00.16	
6th	14.06	01.13	14.07	01.21	
7th	14.17	02.25	14.25	02.27	
8th	14.28	03.40	14.43	03.33	
9th	14.42	04.56	15.04	04.42	
10th	14.59	06.14	15.29	05.52	
11th	15.23	07.34	16.01	07.04	
12th	15.56	08.52	16.40	08.14	full moon
13th	16.43	10.02	17.31	09.20	
14th	17.47	10.59	18.33	10.18	
15th	19.04	11.41	19.45	11.05	
16th	20.30	12.11	21.02	11.43	
17th	21.59	12.33	22.22	12.14	
18th	23.28	12.50	23.42	12.39	
19th	–	13.05	–	13.02	3rd quarter
20th	00.56	13.18	01.01	13.23	
21st	02.24	13.31	02.20	13.45	
22nd	03.52	13.47	03.39	14.08	
23rd	05.20	14.05	04.58	14.35	
24th	06.46	14.30	06.15	15.08	
25th	08.06	15.04	07.28	15.49	
26th	09.15	15.50	08.33	16.38	new moon
27th	10.09	16.49	09.27	17.36	
28th	10.48	17.58	10.11	18.40	
29th	11.16	19.12	10.45	19.47	
30th	11.36	20.27	11.13	20.54	
31st	11.51	21.41	11.35	22.00	

Meteor shower of the month – the Geminids

The year closes with our most spectacular and reliable meteor shower, the Geminids, which is thought to be intensifying each year. This year the peak comes on the night of the 13th and early hours of the 14th, just after the full moon, and so the fainter tracks will be lost, but the Geminids are so bright and numerous that you should catch plenty anyway. There is also no need to get up at pre-dawn to see them, as they are active in the evening – they are at their peak at 02.00 but worth viewing several hours before and after that. The radiant is 70 degrees above the southern horizon at the peak. These meteors are produced when the earth passes through the dust trail left by asteroid 3200 Phaethon, which is named after the son of the Greek sun god Helios, as it has an orbit that takes it closer to the sun than any other named asteroid. Its debris burns up as it hits our atmosphere, producing a beautiful display of slow-moving (and therefore easy to spot) meteors with a yellow hue.

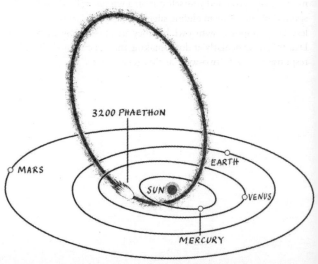

NATURE

Inside the beehive in December

As the shortest day arrives, activity inside the beehive comes almost to a complete halt. Supplies must be eked out, and that means minimal activity (except, perhaps, for hymn singing at midnight on Christmas Eve). The colony forms into the 'winter cluster', a ball-shaped grouping together across several of the hives. The outer bees line up side by side, facing into the cluster, and so creating a thermal layer. Normally this will be one bee thick, but as temperatures drop there can be several layers of insulating bees. Within the cluster the temperature can be mild enough for the bees to move around a little and eat a little honey, and the bees take it in turns to have a spell inside. In really cold weather the cluster will contract, maintaining heat in a small area, and keeping the bees alive until milder days come.

Look out for...short-eared and tawny owls

Short-eared owls are among the few owls to regularly hunt in broad daylight. In winter they move to wetlands and coastal marshes, so if you find yourself out on a winter walk in such a spot, look out for them gliding silently in search of prey. You are less likely to spot a tawny owl, but they are at their noisiest in December, particularly at dusk, making their distinctive call and response 'two-wit' 'two-woo' as they seek a mate.

D

THE GARDEN

Planting by the moon

New moon to 1st quarter: 26th November–4th. Sow crops that develop below ground. Dig the soil.

1st quarter to full moon: 4th–12th. Sow crops that develop above ground. Plant seedlings and young plants.

Full moon to 3rd quarter: 12th–19th. Harvest crops for immediate eating. Harvest fruit.

3rd quarter to new moon: 19th–26th. Prune. Harvest for storage. Fertilise and mulch the soil.

New moon to 1st quarter: 26th–31st. Sow crops that develop below ground. Dig the soil.

Job of the month – pack away for winter

Dahlia tubers need to be lifted, dried off, packed in dry compost or sawdust and stored somewhere frost-free for winter. Chrysanthemum plants should be pruned back, lifted, potted up and moved to a greenhouse or porch. Tender plants now need wrapping in horticultural fleece or bringing indoors, and containers should be given 'pot feet', little pieces of terracotta that lift them from the ground and allow winter rains to drain away.

Glut of the month – beetroot

Beetroot will stand quite happily on the plot all winter – just lift it as you need it. If you have grown colourful yellow and candy-striped varieties as well as the classic deep purple, you have some colourful plates ahead of you.

- **Candy-striped salad:** Chioggia beetroot is beautiful finely sliced with a mandoline as part of a salad with walnuts, leaves and slices of a rosy apple. Dress the salad at the last minute or the pink rings will run.
- **Roast beetroot, carrot and onion:** Cut chunks of beetroot and carrot, and quarter some onions. Roast in extra virgin

olive oil and a good splash of vinegar, at 190°C, Gas Mark 5, turning until all are soft and caramelised.

- **Beetroot broth:** In Poland, this broth, known as *Barszcz Wigilijny*, is often the starter for the traditional supper held at Wigilia (see page 245), eaten once the first star has been spotted. Soften a chopped onion in butter, then add garlic, carrot, celery and diced beetroot, vegetable stock and a splash of vinegar. Cook until all is tender, then season, strain and serve.

Flower of the month – Christmas rose

Latin name: *Helleborus niger* (*Helleborus*, from the Middle English *ellebore* and/or the Greek *helleboros* – a name given to plants that are both poisonous and medicinal; *niger*, Latin for 'black', perhaps referring to the roots).
Common names: hellebore, Christmas rose.

Legend says that the Christmas rose sprouted when the tears of a young girl who had no gift to give the baby Jesus fell on the snow. *Helleborus niger* is certainly as pretty as a snowy Christmas card, with its pure white, simple flowers just begging for a robin to perch nearby – but, in fact, the species does not reliably flower at Christmas and can kick in a little later. Disappointing. However, breeding efforts have been concentrated on bringing that flowering season forward, so if you go to the garden centre this month and buy a hellebore while it is in flower, you should have one that can be decked with outdoor fairy lights every year.

Hellebores do well in the ground, but their downward-facing blooms can get a little lost. They work better in pots that can be lifted up onto tables, or placed either side of the front door for December.

THE KITCHEN

Cheese of the month – Beauvale

Stilton is a winter cheese, and this is the same for Beauvale, a creamy, naturally spreadable Stilton made by traditional Stilton makers Cropwell Bishop in Nottinghamshire. The reason for the timing is the quality of the milk. In August and September the cows have been out all summer and their milk has settled into the perfect combination for blue-cheese making: low in fat but high in protein. (When the fat level is higher – for instance, at the end of winter when the cows have been indoors eating a richer diet – the butterfat restricts the good drainage of the curds that gives a nice smooth and creamy finish, and so the resulting cheese is dry and crumbly.) At the start of maturation, Beauvale likes a warm and humid atmosphere, and so a late-summer start also works perfectly to develop its best flavours. Beauvale needs to mature for 12 weeks, putting this best batch on the table – hopefully with a bottle of port and some crackers – just before Christmas.

In season

Cranberries, satsumas, clementines and **pomegranates** are arriving from southern Europe and the US ahead of Christmas. There are still plenty of home-grown **apples** and **pears**, and some **quince.**

Jerusalem artichokes, carrots, beetroot, leeks, parsnips, cauliflower, Brussels sprouts, kale, winter cabbage are still available, as are stored **maincrop potatoes, borlotti beans** and **winter squash.**

Nuts are plentiful: **hazelnuts, sweet chestnuts** and **walnuts.**

The woody winter herbs – **rosemary, sage** and **bay** – are excellent now.

Black truffles are in season.

Ask specialist butchers for **duck, goose, grouse, guinea fowl, partridge, pheasant, venison** and **wood pigeon.** There is – fairly obviously – lots of **turkey** to be had.

Stilton and **Stichelton** are at their best.

Brill, sardine, skate, clams, mussels and **oysters** are plentiful.

EUROPEAN CHRISTMAS BISCUITS

PEPPARKAKOR
~SWEDEN

PFEFFERNÜSSE
~GERMANY

JOULUTORTTU
~ FINLAND

BRANDY SNAPS
~ENGLAND

PIERNICZKI
~POLAND

RECIPES

Pierniczki w czekoladzie, a recipe by Ren Behan

These star-shaped cookies, filled with plum jam and coated in chocolate, are a traditional, soft variety of gingerbread, eaten at Christmastime by Polish families, sometimes at the end of the Wigilia meal (see page 245). They are best if made ahead, and allowed to soften slightly in a sealed tin. Some cooks place a little piece of apple in the tin to help them soften. They can be decorated with a dark chocolate glaze, as below, or with a thin glaze made with icing sugar and water.

Makes 12 cookies
Ingredients
250ml runny honey
50g butter
1 teaspoon ground ginger
1 teaspoon ground cinnamon
1 teaspoon mixed spice
450g plain flour, plus a little extra for dusting
3 teaspoon baking powder
1 teaspoon cocoa powder
1 egg, lightly beaten

For the filling

120g Polish plum jam (*powidła*) or a very thick marmalade

For the glaze

200g dark chocolate, chopped

1 teaspoon vegetable oil

Method

Preheat the oven to 180°C, Gas Mark 4. In a small pan, very gently heat the honey, butter and spices until just warm. Set to one side to cool. In a large bowl, add the flour, baking powder and cocoa powder, and mix to combine. Add the egg and the cooled honey mixture, and whisk, then bring together with your hands to form a soft dough.

Sprinkle a large board with some flour. Cut the dough into 2 pieces. Take a large sheet of baking paper and roll the dough out on the paper to a thickness of 3mm. If the dough feels sticky, add a little more flour. Using a star-shaped cookie cutter, cut out 12 star shapes (but do not pick up the pieces yet). On each star shape, place ½ teaspoon jam in the centre.

Carefully remove the dough away from the outside of the stars, leaving the star shapes on the baking paper. Set the excess dough to one side. Roll out the rest of the dough to the same thickness, and cut out 12 more star shapes. Cover each star with a corresponding star, enclosing the jam filling. Press the edges down gently to seal each cookie. If you have any dough left over, repeat the process.

Carefully transfer the whole sheet, including the baking paper, onto a large baking tray. Using a clean spray bottle or a pastry brush, spray or brush the cookies with a little water, to help prevent them from drying out. Bake for 12–15 minutes. Cool on a wire rack.

To make the glaze, melt the chocolate in a bowl over a pan of water, and stir in the oil. Pour the chocolate glaze over the cookies on the wire rack to coat them. Once they are cool, place the cookies in a large tin, ideally in one layer, for 2–3 days to allow them to soften.

Borlotti and winter squash casserole with rosemary and cheese dumplings

This is warming, filling, herbal and comforting on a cold night. A Parmesan rind is good for adding rich, savoury flavour to slow-cooked vegetable dishes, so always keep them (they freeze well) when you reach the end of your cheese.

Serves 6

Ingredients

For the casserole

4 tablespoons extra virgin olive oil

1 large onion, diced

Half a butternut squash, peeled and chopped into 5cm chunks

5 cloves garlic, thinly sliced

2 tins cannellini beans, drained (or about 440g cooked beans)

2 tins chopped plum tomatoes

700ml vegetable stock or water

3 bay leaves

A Parmesan rind

½ tablespoon red wine vinegar

100g cavolo nero, leaves stripped from stems and sliced into ribbons

Salt and pepper

For the dumplings

200g self-raising flour

100g grated mature Red Leicester or Cheddar cheese

2 tablespoons finely chopped rosemary

½ teaspoon salt

pepper

About 10 tablespoons water

Method

Preheat the oven to 180°C, Gas Mark 4. In a large casserole on the hob, heat the oil and gently fry the onions until they start to turn translucent. Add the butternut squash and the garlic, and fry for around 10 minutes or until the squash edges start to soften and caramelise. Add the beans, tomatoes, stock or water, bay leaves and Parmesan rind, and bring to the boil. Leave the lid off the casserole and transfer it to the oven. After 50 minutes take it out of the oven and add vinegar, salt and pepper, then taste and add more if needed. Once you are happy with the flavour, mix in the cavolo nero and put the casserole back in the oven while you make the dumplings.

Put the flour, grated cheese, rosemary, salt and pepper into a large mixing bowl and add the water, stirring to combine, but being careful not to overwork. Add a little more water if necessary to bring everything together into a sticky dough. Take the casserole out of the oven and put spoonfuls of the dumpling mixture onto the surface of the stew (try to make even numbers for everyone). Return the uncovered casserole to the oven for about 20–25 minutes, or until the dumplings look well cooked and slightly golden on top. Serve hot.

D

A SONG FOR CHRISTMAS

'The Friendly Beasts'
Traditional

This carol seems to have originated in France but was well
known in England from the 12th century, though this form
of words may be more modern. It lets the animals in the
stable tell their own story of the nativity.

Je - sus our bro - ther, strong and good, was hum - bly

born in a sta - ble rude, and the friend - ly beasts a -

round him stood, Je - sus our bro - ther, strong and good.

'I' said the donkey, shaggy and brown,
'I carried his mother up hill and down;
I carried his mother to Bethlehem town.'
'I' said the donkey, shaggy and brown.

'I' said the cow, all white and red
'I gave him my manger for his bed;
I gave him my hay to pillow his head.'
'I' said the cow, all white and red.

'I' said the sheep with curly horn,
'I gave him my wool for his blanket warm;
He wore my coat on Christmas morn.'
'I' said the sheep with curly horn.

'I' said the dove from the rafters high,
'I cooed him to sleep so that he would not cry;
We cooed him to sleep, my mate and I,'
'I' said the dove from the rafters high.

Thus every beast by some good spell
In the stable dark was glad to tell
Of the gift he gave Emmanuel,
The gift he gave Emmanuel.

REFERENCES

Astronomical and calendarial information reproduced with
permission from HMNAO, UKHO and the Controller of
Her Majesty's Stationery Office.

Moon and sun rises and sets and further calculations reproduced
with permission from www.timeanddate.com.

Tidal predictions reproduced with permission from HMNAO,
UKHO and the Controller of Her Majesty's Stationery Office.

Planetary predictions are derived from the DE405 ephemeris,
which is produced by NASA's Jet Propulsion Laboratory (JPL)
in California.

Weather averages reproduced with permission from
www.holiday-weather.com.

Sea temperatures are reproduced with permission from
www.seatemperature.org.

FURTHER READING

Websites

Tides – www.ukho.gov.uk/easytide
Frost dates – www.plantmaps.com
Snow crystals identification – www.snowcrystals.com
Bees through the year – gabrielshoneyfarm.co.uk;
www.paulacarnell.com
Months in the languages of the British Isles – jakubmarian.com

Books

Harris, J. and Rickards, J., *Moon Gardening*, London: John Blake
Publishing, 2016

Hartley, D., *Food in England*, London: Piatkus, 2009

Jones, J. and Deer, B., *Cattern Cakes and Lace*, London: Dorling
Kindersley, 1991

Koch, J. T. (ed.), *Celtic Culture: Aberdeen Breviary-Celticism,* Santa
Barbara: ABC-CLIO, 2006

Thomson, W., *The Book of Tides*, London: Quercus, 2016

Watson, M. L., *The Biology of the Honey Bee,* Cambridge Mass:
Harvard University Press, 1991

ACKNOWLEDGEMENTS

Thank you to the many people who have contributed thoughts, ideas, knowledge and hard work to creating *The Almanac 2019*. To my dad, Jack Leendertz, for meticulous work on the Sky at Night sections and – very excitingly – for creating our very own software to produce predictions. To my step dad, John Read, for guidance on how best to include tidal information. To the cheese makers and cheesemongers! Alison Blunt at Golden Cross Cheese; Debbie Courat of Lynher Dairies; Nathan Coyte of Neal's Yard Dairy; Stephen Fletcher at Ram Hall Farm; Mary Holbrook of Sleight Farm; Becky Holden of Hafod Cheese; Angela Homewood of Homewood Cheeses; Rosie Morgan of Bristol Cheesemonger; all at Trethowan's Dairy, Westcombe Dairy, Hampshire Cheeses, Leicestershire Cheese and Cropwell Bishop. To Paula Carnell for her wisdom on bees.

I am delighted to be including recipes written for the almanac by Li Ling Wang, Josephine Haller and Ren Behan. And thanks to Claire Thomson and Matt Williamson, Tamar Lucas, and Diana Henry respectively, for introducing us. Thank you to Ian Curley and Karen Millar for your diligent work setting the scores for the folk songs.

The Almanac would be half the book it is without Matt Cox of Newman+Eastwood's clear, calm, beautiful design. We have both loved working with Celia Hart, this year's illustrator, who has brought the book alive with her instinctive understanding of the turning of the year.

Thanks to all the brilliant people at Octopus: Ella Parsons, Jonathan Christie, Caroline Brown, Kevin Hawkins, Ellen Bashford, Karen Baker, Megan Brown, Matthew Grindon, Lauren Mitchell, Alison Wormleighton, Jane Birch and of course the wonderful Stephanie Jackson, irrepressible almanac cheerleader and steadiest possible hand on the tiller.

To Cerys Matthews for being such a champion of *The Almanac* and for giving me the opportunity to come along to BBC 6 Music every month and talk about the the seasons.

Thank you to my wonderful family – Michael, Rowan and Meg – who once again had to put up with my near-absence through an intensive period of writing and research. Thanks also to friends and family who supported us, particularly my mum, Cath Read.

Finally, thank you again to the community of people who supported the first edition of *The Almanac*. You launched me on this path and I never forget it.

INDEX

ABOUT THE AUTHOR

Lia Leendertz is an award-winning garden and food writer. She contributes regularly to the *Guardian*, the *Telegraph*, *Gardens Illustrated*, *The Garden* and *Simple Things* magazine. She is the author of several gardening books and the cookbook *Petal, Leaf, Seed: Cooking with the treasures of the garden*. Lia has a monthly almanac spot on BBC Radio 6 Music with Cerys Matthews.

Find out more about Lia at:
www.lialeendertz.com
Twitter: @lialeendertz
Instagram: @lia_leendertz

ABOUT THE ILLUSTRATOR

Celia Hart is an illustrator and printmaker living and working on the Suffolk/Cambridgeshire border. She works without a press, producing hand-burnished linocuts – she enjoys using the negative and positive shapes and the marks of the chisels to create depth and variety in the composition.

For more information visit Celia's web site:
www.celiahart.co.uk